D1346156

MEN AGAINST TANKS

MEN AGAINST TANKS

A History of Anti-Tank Warfare

JOHN WEEKS

DAVID & CHARLES

NEWTON ABBOT LONDON VANCOUVER

ISBN 0 7153 6909 1

© John Weeks 1975

All rights reserved. No part of this publication
may be reproduced, stored in a retrieval system,
or transmitted, in any form or by any means,
electronic, mechanical, photocopying, recording
or otherwise, without the prior permission
of David & Charles (Publishers) Limited

Set in 11 on 13pt Imprint and printed
in Great Britain
by Latimer Trend & Company Ltd Plymouth
for David & Charles (Holdings) Limited
South Devon House Newton Abbot Devon

Published in Canada
by Douglas David & Charles Limited
132 Philip Avenue North Vancouver BC

CONTENTS

LIST OF
ILLUSTRATIONS

Grateful acknowledgements are made to the following for permission to reproduce photographs used in this volume which are listed above:

British Aircraft Corporation: 27
Mrs Robert Goddard: 29
Hoffschmidt Collection: 7, 10, 13A, 30
Imperial War Museum, London: 1, 2, 3, 5, 11
Redstone Arsenal: 14
US Army: 8, 12, 15, 16, 24
West Point Museum: 6A–C, 13A–D, 20A

All the other plates are reproduced from photographs in the author's collection.

DIAGRAMS

7

INTRODUCTION

An expert is a man who knows more and more about less and less.

Nicholas Murray Butler

There is one name missing from the list of acknowledgements to those who helped me in the writing of this book. It is the name of the man who first gave me the idea. It came about like this. Many years ago I went into the film theatre at the School of Infantry to see some training films. Half-way through the afternoon an old, scratched copy of a World War II German training film was thrown on the screen. It dealt with the methods that should be used by infantry in attacking tanks. The date was probably 1943 or 1944; the methods were simple, involving much bravery to be successful; the action was fast and the whole film most exciting. It was called *Männer gegen Panzer*, or *Men against Tanks*, and the title has stuck in my mind ever since. The film has now gone and I shall never know the name of the producer who so inspired me, but he has my deepest respect and gratitude, as do the various soldiers who took part in the film. From that day sprang my interest in this important, but often maligned subject.

The story of anti-tank combat is probably the briefest in the entire history of warfare, for it is even shorter than that of aerial fighting. It begins in 1917 when aeroplane combat was already two years old and when submarines, radios, and similar modern devices were already in general use. Until the end of World War I it was an entirely one-sided conflict with the tanks solely on the Allied side and the anti-tank expertise solely on the German side. A certain amount of progress was made by both combatants but

9

there was really nothing very startling. It was just enough to make the point that here was something which would have to be studied in preparing for all future wars.

The 1920s and early 1930s were a doldroms period for anti-tank warfare in every meaning of the word. Army staffs virtually ignored the matter, behaving to some extent rather like ostrichs when caught in the open, and a great deal of valuable time was frittered away which had to be made up later on. The British Experimental Armoured Force of 1929 was a remarkable step forward in the thinking behind the use of armoured vehicles, but when one reads the reports of it, one has to look very hard indeed to find any mention of anti-tank measures in any shape or form. There are a few references to engineer works such as mines and obstacles, but by and large the subject was ignored.

At this time there were no specific anti-tank guns in service anywhere in the British, French, American, or Russian armies and all these major countries were content to leave the entire subject in the hands of private industry. The manufacturers, struggling to keep themselves afloat in the face of recessions, pacifism and military cutbacks, were not always entirely aware of the military requirement, and they produced a range of largely similar guns all of surprising feebleness and similarity of calibre.

Most of the European armies tried these little guns in one form or another but were very wary of adopting them. Britain toyed with an Oerlikon 20mm and even put it on a tracked trailer to tow behind the minuscule Carden-Lloyd carrier, but nothing came of the idea. The Danes and the Dutch tried their own native designs: but one has the impression that their hearts were never in the work and, with no money in the budget, the projects came to naught.

Apart from the desperate financial shortages there were other reasons for the stagnation of anti-tank thought. The armour plate on tanks had made very few advances between 1918 and 1936 so that the weapon that had been good enough to go through the side of a Mark IV at Messines was very likely to do the same to the 1934 model. The designers were not faced with much of a challenge and the ability to penetrate only one inch of hard armour plate was considered good enough for any gun. Also, trench warfare, or at least some form of static warfare, was expected in the next war as in 1918, and once again artillery pieces would be able to account for most of the tank attacks. So the subject was pushed away to the edge of the desk underneath the coffee cups and the Pending basket. Unfortunately, the Spanish Civil War did not do much to help forward thinking, although there were some stirrings among the Axis Powers, and it was not until the blitzkrieg in France that the full realisation burst. By the greatest good fortune both sides were equally badly off and the remainder of World War II was spent in a desperate race between anti-tank guns and tanks. This was the period of real progress in anti-tank warfare and it makes for fascinating and hectic reading.

Now there was no lack of money for any project but frequently there was little or no factory space in which to build the various designs. The Allies found it necessary to stick to a few simple models which were usually outdated almost as soon as they came into service. The German Army on the other hand chased all manner of different ideas, with varying success, to produce a variety and range which has rarely been seen in any other field of armament. After 1945 the captured records of German research were used on both sides of the Iron Curtain as a basis for the modern families of weapons.

This book sets out to tell this crowded and remarkable story from the beginning to the present day – but it tells it only in part. As the title suggests, this is the story of men fighting machines, and the equipment which those men use. This self-imposed restriction has meant that the story has been built around those anti-armour weapons which are carried, pulled, or pushed by men on their feet. The armoured vehicle and the self-propelled gun have been entirely left out, for that is a specialised subject of great depth which is adequately covered by other writers. The complicated war of obstacles, mines, ditches and similar engineering construction has also been ignored since this is another study entirely and one which does not lend itself either to easy writing or to easy reading. At times the author has seen fit to stray into one or two other fields, such as aircraft, since they follow the logical line of thought of the mobility of battlefield weapons, but basically this is the story of the infantryman and his fight against the tank.

Every subject has its technical language and anti-tank warfare is no exception. It may perhaps assist the reader who is unfamiliar with the technical terms to offer a brief explanation of the ways and means that have been and are used in the fighting of tanks. In fact there is nothing very unusual that is employed and the general intention in all cases is to defeat the protection offered by the armour on the vehicle. Broadly speaking, this is attempted in three ways: firstly, by setting the vehicle on fire; secondly, by shattering the armour by detonating a large explosive charge on the side of the vehicle; and finally, by punching a hole through the armour plate.

Setting fire to an armoured vehicle is not particularly easy although there have been spectacular successes in the past. As a general method of attack incendiarism was little used after 1942, although the modern use of napalm looks as though it might be a worthwhile approach. But modern tanks do not burn easily and no great effort has been made.

Shattering the armoured plate by large quantities of explosives can be quite a successful way of attacking a tank, but for an infantryman it isn't an easy matter to make the preliminary arrangements. Explosive is heavy to carry and tanks are very difficult to approach; frequently they are accompanied by their own infantry. However, this method has been used many times in the past and the modern 'Squash-Head' shell is an extension of the idea.

Most of the effort in anti-tank weapons is channelled into the different ways of making holes in armoured plate. The oldest and still the most successful method is to fire a solid chunk of very hard metal which by sheer energy and momentum punches its way through the armour. The design of such projectiles is a very exact and difficult science but it does follow a few general rules. Firstly, the projectile has to travel very fast and this means a high-velocity gun, and so a large muzzle blast and considerable recoil. Next the projectile needs to be as heavy as possible and as hard as possible. Finally, it has to strike the target at the correct angle or it will bounce off. To reduce the bounce, a soft cap of malleable metal is put on the nose and this acts as a sort of 'shock absorber' and in effect 'sticks' the nose to the armour for a fraction of a second so that it can start to punch through. This shock absorber is known as an armour-piercing cap. To work properly the cap has to be very blunt, and to reduce air drag a second cap is put on top of it which is carefully streamlined. The result is a rather complicated and quite expensive solid shot which goes by the name of Armour Piercing Capped Ballistic Cap, or APCBC, and this string of letters crops up quite frequently in the description of anti-tank ammunition.

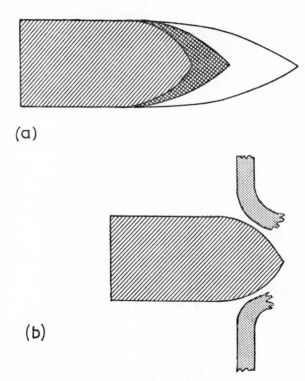

(a)

(b)

a Armour-piercing shell with cap and ballistic cap (APCBC).
b The solid shot of the shell pushes a hole in the armour and the two
caps disappear.

The simplest way to get greater speed from the projectile is simply to put more powder in the chamber. This of course increases the recoil in direct proportion, and in World War II a great deal of effort was directed towards ways of gaining speed without gaining recoil. The German approach, which is described in more detail later, was to taper the barrel and so squeeze the shot out at a greater velocity than it would have got from a parallel bore. The British toyed with a version of this idea but quickly dropped it. Another method which in effect does the same thing is to make up a composite projectile consisting of a small solid core surrounded by much lighter pieces of packing which build it up to the right size to fit the barrel. When the projectile is fired, the lighter packing falls away at the muzzle and the solid core travels to the target at a very much higher speed than if it had been a full-

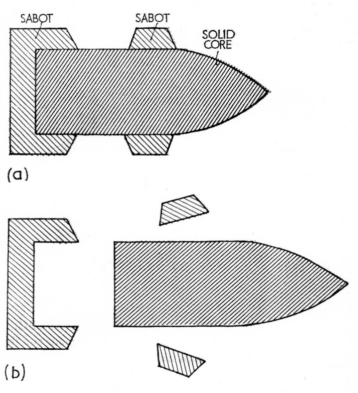

(a)

(b)

a   Armour-piercing discarding sabot shot (APDS): the shell is loaded as one piece, the sabots being stuck to it. It travels up the barrel as a unit, the sabots providing the gas seal and gripping the rifling. At the muzzle the sabots fall away.
b   APDS discarding at the muzzle.

14

sized shot. This system is known as the Armour Piercing Discarding Sabot or APDS and was introduced by the British towards the end of World War II. It greatly improved the performance of the feebler anti-tank guns then in service, and is still the best method of attacking tanks.

But firing a hard solid projectile is beyond the capacity of most infantry weapons and well beyond the capacity of any man-carried weapon. The best method for light weapons, indeed the only method, is to use a hollow-charge explosive. Hollow charge works by a strange phenomenon which is still not entirely understood. Originally known as the Monro Effect, the history of which is outlined in a later chapter, the present hollow-charge

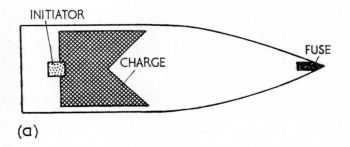

(a)

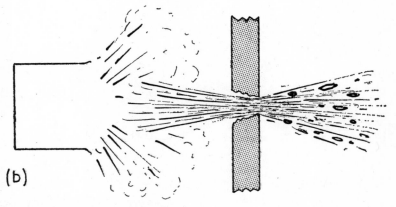

(b)

a   Typical hollow-charge shell.
b   The shaped charge of the shell opposite forms a jet which burns
through armour.

munition consists of a cylindrical block of explosive which has a conical hole in one end. This conical hole has an effect rather like an optical lense in that it concentrates all the explosive force in one direction and produces an immensely powerful narrow column or jet which moves with much more force and speed than does a plain explosive wave. Even more power can be obtained by lining the cone with a thin layer of a soft metal such as copper so that molten copper is carried with the jet. The effect of this jet is that it both melts the armour plate and blows it away by sheer explosive force. The results can be quite remarkable. A small charge of less than $\frac{1}{2}$lb, when properly designed and detonated at the right distance, can make a hole in a piece of armour 9in or 10in thick. Hence quite small rockets can knock out very large tanks and it is the hollow charge which has made possible the whole present generation of infantry anti-tank weapons.

So much then for the preliminaries. In the following chapters the technical complications have been reduced to their simplest possible form and those readers for whom technicalities and jargon induce mental indigestion need not feel that they will be subjected to much discomfort. The story can at all times be followed without the necessity for understanding the fine detail. In essence it is a straightforward account of the combat between men on their feet and men in bullet-proof machines.

(*Opposite, top*) The crew of a British tank examining a German Mauser anti-tank rifle. This photograph shows the considerable length of the weapon; (*opposite, centre*) A Carden–Lloyd tractor towing a 20mm Oerlikon anti-tank gun, taken in 1929 or 1930. This little vehicle and its gun might have been a useful combination at that time, but within a few years it was too feeble to defeat tanks; (*opposite, bottom*) The British 2-pounder, anti-tank gun and crew. A beautifully made gun, it was unfortunately obsolete by the start of World War II.

Page 18 (*above*) The Northover projector, one of the smooth-bore guns introduced 1940–1 for the Home Guard. The breech is open, ready for loading, and the tall backsight is set up for aiming; (*below*) The Home Guard Smith gun, another smooth-bore weapon of 1941. It was remarkable for its unconventional way of being brought into action.

I

EARLY DAYS

Everything was affected by the fearful impression that the fire-
vomiting iron dragons had on artillery and infantry . . .

German battalion war diary, August 1918

The external features of the first British tanks are well enough
known not to need more than a cursory explanation – two large
rhomboidal sides with tracks running around them, and a rec-
tangular box in between containing the crew and engine. Guns
were carried in sponsons on the side and other armament was
mounted in the front or rear plates. The 'male' tank had two
ex-naval 6-pounder guns, one in each sponson, and four Hotchkiss or Lewis machine-guns. The 'female' was armed with six
machine-guns. These tanks had a maximum speed of 3·5mph
and were good at crossing trenches. They had no springs in their
suspension, nor sound-proofing in any part of the internal lining.
The inside of the crew compartment was enormous by present-
day standards with the engine standing upright in the forward
half of the floor and its gearbox behind it. The crew was eight
men, four of them gunners who sat in the sponsons. Of the
other four, one was the commander, in front on the left-hand
seat; one was the driver, alongside the commander; and two were
gearsmen. Gearsmen were positioned on each side of the engine
and gearbox and they changed the gears according to the hand
signals given to them by the driver.

A moving tank was generally sheer hell inside. The engine
quickly heated up the interior to 90° F or more. The Rickardo
engine was notoriously smoky and fumes poured from it to fill
the inside with an eye-stinging smoke which made the head

ache and the throat sore. The noise was indescribable and exhausting. Not only was the engine bare and exposed, but the gear wheels had straight teeth which screamed and groaned, the tracks clanked and rattled in a steady ear-shattering accompaniment which came from floor, ceiling and sides at the same time. Normal voice communication was impossible and hand signals were often difficult to see in the semi-darkness where the only light came through the ports and vision slits. There are several accounts of actions in which the tanks were unable to follow up an advantage, or to respond to orders to move, simply because the crews were physically beyond any further effort, worn out by their machines.

Only the driver and commander had any idea of where the tank was and where it was going, and often the driver's knowledge was restricted to looking a few yards away at the next obstacle. The gunners would catch glimpses from time to time of the outside world and they would select targets and engage them. But only too often, if the commander wanted a particular gun to fire at some target chosen by him, he had to leave his seat and crawl down to the gun position and show the gunner where to fire. Shooting was possible when on the move since the top speed was so low and it was not too difficult to get a snap shot as the tank heaved and swayed along. Naturally the firing added to the discomfort and noise inside, as well as producing cordite fumes to mix with the others already present.

There was no forced ventilation, and fresh air had to find its way in as best it could. Entrance and exit was by means of small doors in the sides and hatches in the roof. These never fitted very well and were difficult to crawl through in either direction. To drag a wounded man out from a tank was both hard work for the rescuers and painful for the rescued. There was no padding or other protection for the crew, and minor injuries were common from being thrown against the numerous corners and projections as the vehicle heaved its way across the broken ground.

The first models had small periscopes for viewing but these were quickly discarded when it was found that there was a very real danger of the glass shattering and flying into the viewer's face under small-arms attack. An attempt to use polished metal surfaces as mirrors failed and crude slits in the armour were all that could be offered, with serious effects upon the morale of the crews in later actions.

In the first action on the Somme on 15 September 1916 the tanks pretty well had it their own way as far as human opposition was concerned. Fifty-nine had been sent to France under conditions of total secrecy so that their appearance on the battlefield was a complete and demoralising surprise to the Germans. Ten were so bad mechanically that they were left in the rear as a 'reserve', thirty-two reached the Start Line, fourteen left the Start Line on time, nine left it later, five became stuck in the mud during the attack, and nine completed their task. A success ratio of 15 per cent is hardly impressive, but that partial success was highly encouraging and it ensured that the idea of the tank was supported by the generals. In this first tank battle, the enemy was the tank's own mechanical unreliability, for most had been practically worn out in training their crews in England before being shipped to France. Only two are recorded as having encountered opposition and it is significant that this opposition was from field guns. Near Gudecourt a tank disabled a 77mm gun but was then knocked out itself. Another caught fire from a direct hit but returned safely. This first action was not a complete success, but it was highly encouraging for the British and two smaller attacks in the closing months of 1916 were equally worthwhile.

For the Germans the appearance of the tanks was a surprise which they took some time to get over. These early tank attacks owed as much to morale for their successes as they did to material destruction or tactical manoeuvre. When the matter is analysed, the reasons why the morale factor assumed such proportions are not hard to find. Here, for the first time in history, the great characteristic of mobility, together with fire-power and protection, had been successfully combined to produce a self-contained offensive unit the like of which had never before been seen in any war. The approach of these monsters, seen through the eyes of a front-line infantryman, presented a personal problem which had to be solved immediately. He had three choices: to stop the tank, to surrender, or to leave his position. He had no past experience to fall back on, and no training to help him. His weapons were apparently useless against the oncoming machine and his companions were no better placed than he. In the circumstances one cannot be surprised that many chose the second and third alternatives. Not surprisingly the Germans were at first inclined to look upon tanks as unfair weapons. After the first action on the Somme the chief of staff of the German Third Army Group reported that: 'The enemy, in the latest fighting, has employed new engines of war as cruel as they are effective.'

But the German Army learned quickly. The next attacks with tanks were not until the spring of 1917, when they were in any case only partially successful as a result of lack of proper training, the muddy ground and poor co-ordination with the infantry. In this battle, for the first time, the infantry struck back. The German machine-gunners, and some snipers, had been issued with a special type of rifle ammunition since 1915. This was known as 'K' type. The 'K' bullet was heavier than the normal one and had a tungsten-carbide core. Each round was carefully made and the weight of the bullet and the quantity of propellant exactly matched so that all rounds had a similar muzzle-velocity and a similar trajectory. They were used for precise shooting against long-range targets and also against protected targets. The heavy tungsten-cored bullet flew very accurately to longer ranges than the normal lead-cored one, and so gave the sniper an advantage out to 800yd or more. At closer ranges it would penetrate the thin sheet-steel plates which were used to protect sentries and lookouts in the front-line trenches. At Arras it was found that the 'K' bullet also went through the armour of the Mark I and Mark II tanks. In both models the plating was suicidally thin. It varied from 0·2 to 0·4in and was made from the relatively soft metal known to the trade as 'boiler plate'. However, the limitations of the boiler plate were not revealed to the German High Command until two days later. Then, at Bullecourt on 11 April 1917, a spirited German counter-attack captured two tanks and immediately the effect of the 'K' bullet was discovered. All German infantrymen were thereupon issued with five rounds of 'K' ammunition for attacking tanks, and machine-gunners were given a complete belt of it.

However, the British had also noted the penetrating power of the 'K' and had called for hardened armour on the next mark of tank. Another feature which struck the Germans was the damage inflicted on the tank crew by bullet splash from ordinary rifle and machine-gun fire. The early tanks were full of holes, both large and small. Badly fitting doors, spy holes, vision slits, gun ports, pistol ports – all left a multitude of gaps and through these gaps there came hot, molten lead. When a lead-cored bullet hit the outside of the armour, it flattened and squeezed out its lead core in a 'splash' which radiated in a circular pattern. Under the force of the impact, the lead became nearly liquid and spread out with almost explosive velocity. At a range of a foot, bullet splash is very nearly lethal, and the fast-moving liquid lead will force its way through any crack that presents itself. The tank crews quickly began to suffer casualties from splash entering the slits and joints in the armour, nearly all of them occurring to the gunners and commanders. The morale effect was quite serious, and a crude form of face armour was tried in an effort to overcome the problem. This armour consisted of a pair of goggles and a face shield of chain mail sewn on leather, hung from a lightweight helmet. The idea was sound enough, but nobody could wear it and fight at the same time; the goggles misted up and the leather hood was unbearably hot. The crews preferred to take their chance.

In Messines in June 1917 the first Mark IVs were used, and these had armour which successfully withstood the 'K' bullet. Realising this, the Germans immediately put a programme in hand which was to result in the first infantry anti-tank weapon ever to be produced. The task was given to the firm of Mauser and they solved it by scaling up the standard infantry 7·92mm rifle to a calibre of 13mm. Special ammunition had to be made for it since none existed in that size, and the Mauser factory had to install extra machinery to make the big rifle. However, progress was rapid and the Mauser 'T' rifle was in service within a year. 'T' stood for 'Tank' and the German nomenclature for the rifle was 'Tank-Gewehr', usually shortened to 'T-Gew'. It was 67in long and weighed 26lb, resembling the Model 98 rifle almost exactly, except for the length of the barrel, which was out of scale, and a pistol grip, which had to be fitted to the small of the butt. Obviously a rifle as long as this could not be held and fired in the normal way, and a light bipod was fitted to the front of the stock. The breech was closed by a rotating bolt of identical pattern to the 7·92mm rifle, but there was no magazine. Single rounds were fed into the breech by hand. At 120yd the bullet penetrated the Mark IV armour provided that it struck at right angles, but at 45° it would not go through the thinnest plate of the Mark IV, even at a range of 60yd. The recoil was considerable, and one report says that troops were unwilling to use the gun; but popular or not, it was effective and many hundreds were issued.

Another German anti-tank weapon was the light trench mortar. A new carriage was designed for the standard trench mortar with excellent results to enable it to fire at low angle. Naturally the mortar had to be outside a trench to fire, but by skilful siting, this was easily managed. It is likely that some of the tank losses attributed to shell fire might more properly be credited to trench mortars as this translation from a German document of 21 August 1918 shows:

> In two divisions, light trench mortars employed for anti-tank defences have done excellent work. In one of these divisions the results do not permit of exact analysis because the fire of artillery, trench mortars and machine guns was employed simultaneously. The other division, the 192nd, made the following report:
>
> (1)   Tanks of which the armour had been pierced caught fire. It seems that neither the plates on the sides nor those on the turret were reinforced.
>
> (2)   The fire was accurate up to 500 metres. Up to that distance it is certain that the tank will be destroyed. At longer ranges (500 to 800 metres) the fire of light trench mortars was very effective: the tanks were forced to turn back . . .

The same report goes on to say that the suppressive fire of tank machine-guns is only accurate at ranges of 300m or less, which seems to indicate that a trench-mortar crew could outrange a female tank by 200yd or more and destroy it without danger to themselves.

The greatest danger to the World War I tank was the field gun. No tank could survive a hit from a field gun, and there was no hope of keeping out the shells. The Mark Is and IVs were over

20ft long and 8ft high with vertical sides. To have put proper armour on such a huge area would have added many tons to what was already a rather overloaded vehicle, and the principles of sloped armour were some years away for land vehicles. The German 77mm M 1896 was an ideal anti-tank gun. It was reasonably light by the standards of the day and it fired a 15lb shell, one of which could destroy a tank entirely. The Germans quickly learned to deploy these guns well forward in mutually supporting positions where they could not only deal with advancing tanks, but could fill in the waiting time by being useful close-support artillery also. However, care was taken not to use them too much in support roles lest they be knocked out by counter-battery fire before the battle began. Each division also detailed off a section of field guns from its reserve units and kept them limbered up, with their horses in readiness, in case of an urgent alert. These guns carried steel-pointed, armour-piercing shell in their limbers and were an immediate 'Flying Squad' for any threatened area. Excellent though these arrangements were, they imposed an extra strain on the artillery and, more seriously, the number of guns available for conventional fire tasks was cut down.

The history of the Royal Tank Regiment is full of accounts of tanks being engaged by German field guns and one effect of many of these actions was that the tank was usually set alight. The early machines carried their petrol in two large tanks in the forward half of the fighting compartment, one on each side. A hit anywhere in this area was enough to cause incineration. Probably the best-known occasion of field guns defeating a tank assault was the attack on Flesquières during the First Battle of Cambrai on 20 November 1917. The tanks of E Battalion were separated from their following infantry and, as they came over a small ridge outside the village, ran into heavy and accurate fire from several batteries of guns which had been specially set aside for anti-tank work. Sixteen tanks were knocked out in rapid succession, five of them by a bold underofficer named Kruger who served one gun single-handed and gained himself a reputation so resounding that he was actually mentioned in Haig's despatch for that day. He figures also in the official history of the campaign as the 'Flesquières Gunner'. The sad part of the story is that this slaughter should never have occurred, for it was known that the guns were there, and No 64 Squadron RFC (Sopwith Camels) was given the task of finding them and strafing them with machine-gun fire and 20lb Cooper bombs before the battle started, but the guns were so carefully hidden that in three days of searching only one or two were located. Had the infantry been up with the tanks, they might have been able to overrun the guns before too much damage had been done. It was a sharp lesson, though the price was high to the Germans also, for all the guns were captured.

But tank casualties came not only from guns alone. The Germans quickly grasped that every soldier must be prepared to attack tanks and by the middle of 1918 special anti-tank forts were constructed on the likely tank approaches through a position. These forts were relatively simple affairs, containing as many anti-tank rifles and mortars as could be gathered, together with a few field guns. The troops who manned these redoubts were specially trained in attacking tanks and were expected to use every possible means to stop them. There are several accounts of German soldiers swarming over the tanks and firing pistols into the available openings. In other cases, bundles of hand-grenades were placed on top of the roof and the plating blown in. In one or two instances, infantry actually grasped the tank machine-guns and tried to pull them out of the hull. One tank was defeated by phosphorous grenades which choked the crew. Ludendorff placed great emphasis on tank destruction and an order on 21 August 1918 announced that the individuals who distinguished themselves in action against tanks would be mentioned in the Daily Communique and awarded distinctions.

For the Allies the problem was nowhere near so pressing. The Germans built only about twenty of their own design of tank and captured about another dozen. These were used in small numbers in support of infantry assaults on ten or eleven occasions. The results were roughly the same as for the British – the infantry in the trenches were more or less helpless against them, but whenever field guns appeared, the tanks were knocked out. However, conscious that this situation might not continue, the British introduced a novel tank-killer – a rifle-launched, anti-armour grenade. This was the No 44 grenade, accepted for service in April 1918. It had a cylindrical tin body containing 11·5oz of amatol and a contact fuze. It was a rodded grenade, which means that it had a short steel rod screwed into the base, which the firer pushed into the muzzle of his rifle. A blank cartridge was used to propel it. In flight the grenade was steadied by a cloth 'skirt' which trailed behind and made sure that it arrived nose-first. Very little is known about this grenade, probably no more than 15,000 or 20,000 were made, and less than 10,000 were left in 1919. It was then withdrawn from service. How effective it was is not recorded, nor whether it was ever used in action. It seems unlikely that so small an amount of explosive would have had much effect upon a tank, particularly since the Germans found it necessary to tie several of their stick grenades together into a bundle before they made any impression on armour. The chief claim to fame for the No 44 is that it was the first of a long line of anti-tank grenades – a line which is still in existence and flourishing.

The French never made much effort to produce a special anti-tank weapon. They already had a small gun which could suffice in an emergency, the Model 1916 37mm Puteaux, the first of a series of 37mm guns destined to last for almost thirty years. The Puteaux had originally been designed by a Major Garnier in 1886 as a light infantry-support gun. It was put on one side until trench warfare started in 1915 and the French infantry demanded a means of knocking out machine-gun nests. The little Puteaux was good enough for that sort of job and with a solid shot it could punch a hole in thin armour, provided the range was reasonably short. It weighed 340lb and looked much like a miniature 75mm, even down to the Nordenfelt breech, split trail and shield. When the US Army entered the war, it took on the Puteaux and built it under licence in the USA; by the time of the Armistice, 600 were in service in France and 884 had been built altogether. It seems highly unlikely that any of these guns was ever used in action against a tank and they were quickly phased out after the war and stored in arsenals.

The end of the war brought about an immediate stop to any anti-tank activities and throughout the 1920s there was little if any further progress. The formation of the Experimental Mechanised Force in 1927 on Salisbury Plain did much to draw attention to the need for properly constituted armoured formations, but anti-armour tactics were scarcely touched on. Despite the fact that tanks had advanced a little, the anti-tank weapons were hardly any different from those of 1918. By 1930 this had changed for the better, and in the next two years improved still further. Several arms firms took an interest in the matter and a variety of guns began to appear on the market. The strange feature of the majority of them was an almost slavish uniformity of calibre, no matter what the nationality. At the bottom end of the scale was the 20mm range, offered by Solothurn and Oerlikon in Switzerland, Madsen in Denmark, HAIHA in Holland, and Becker in France. All were automatic, feeding their ammunition from magazines for the most part. The average armour penetration was between 0·6 and 1in at 400yd, depending upon the manufacturer's interpretation of his firing trials. The British Army tried the Oerlikon and mounted it on a small tracked trailer, towed by a Carden-Lloyd carrier. It cannot have been a success since it was never adopted.

The next size was 37mm and in 1933 there were eight of these to be found: from Armstrong in Britain, Bofors in Sweden, Maklen and Rosenberg in Russia, the Puteaux in France, the M2E1 in the USA (a version of the Puteaux), the M 1922 in Japan, and the Skoda in Czechoslovakia. All weighed between 200 and 700lb, all fired a shell weighing more than 1lb 8oz and less than 2lb, and all except one claimed an armour penetration of just over an inch at 1,000yd. The exception was the Armstrong which could only achieve the same penetration at 300yd, but in its favour was the fact that it was the lightest gun in the group. The US M2E1 was an improved Puteaux with better ammunition and a sliding-block breech to take the strain of the greater pressures. All except the Japanese M 1922 resembled miniature field guns, with a trail, shield, and wheels. The M 1922 had no wheels and the barrel was supported on a light tripod very similar to that of a machine-gun. As a result, stability was marginal and muzzle-velocity low. There is some reason to believe that the ammunition for this gun was the same as for the Puteaux and, if this is true, it is likely that its performance was even worse than the Armstrong. However, the Japanese were secretive about the full details.

Finally, there were the 47mm guns. There were five of these on the market, from Beardmore and Vickers in Britain, Bofors in Sweden, HAIHA in Holland and Poczisk in Poland. Once again they were all depressingly similar in their dimensions and claimed performance, which was not noticeably better than the 37mm variety. Of these only the Vickers was adopted for service and a limited number were mounted in tanks where they were called 3-pounders.

There was also a revival of interest in the anti-tank rifle. Poland was the first country to design one and the Mauser T-Gew of 1918 was quite obviously the base from which the inspiration was drawn. The Marosczek, as the resulting rifle was called, was a considerable improvement over the Mauser. For one thing, it was lighter – in fact, the lightest anti-tank rifle ever produced. It weighed 19·5lb and the recoil was kept within acceptable limits by using a small bullet and a large cartridge case to give a very high velocity. The case was very similar to that of the Mauser, but it was sharply necked down to take a 7·92mm bullet with a tungsten-carbide core. At 300yd this bullet could penetrate ¾in of armour plate, at least as good a performance as the 20mm machine-guns provided. There was, of course, a price to pay: the barrel wore out rapidly and 200 rounds was the average life with full-power ammunition. For training and instructional firing a reduced-power cartridge was used which allowed an almost unlimited barrel-life. When it was introduced in 1935, the Marosczek was well ahead of anything in service in any other country and it caused considerable interest. In Britain its virtues were seen at once and within a year a design team set to work to build a similar rifle using the same principles. There are good grounds for believing that the Germans did the same.

One year later the Spanish Civil War started and the dictatorships quickly took sides and sent in troops and equipment under various disguises. Within a few months tanks had appeared and were used in action. There were never enough to allow large formations to manoeuvre, but there were certainly sufficient to try out the various types and their weapons. The same was true for anti-tank weapons, where they existed. The Spaniards had none and the best they could buy were some 25mm Hotchkiss and 37mm Improved Puteaux from France. The Hotchkiss was quickly proved to be useless for its shot bounced off every tank that appeared. In fact, the Hotchkiss had a worse performance than the 20mm Oerlikon, which fired a lighter round. The 37mm was better, but only marginally effective. However, because it did actually penetrate the sides and back of some of the smaller tanks, particularly the Italian ones, it gained a reputation that was to lead the French Army into some grief a few years later. The Germans sent six companies of anti-tank guns, together with their gunners. These were 37mm PAK 36 guns, a native design which owed little to any other nationality and a substantial advance on any other 37mm gun. It was small, light and fired a 1·5lb shot at 2,700ft/sec – sufficient to penetrate most armour of the day. With skilful handling the PAK 36 became well-liked by its own side, and feared by the opposition. This, as with the French and their 37mm, was to work to the detriment of the German Army when World War II started, for the PAK 36 was not all that good.

Out-gunned, out-manoeuvred, and hard-pressed, the Spanish had no effective answer to the tank; in desperation they resorted to hand-to-hand fighting. Men lay in ditches and trenches until the tanks were almost upon them, and then leapt out and climbed on top, firing into vision ports, jamming crow-bars into hatch covers and gun mantlets, and pouring petrol into the engine compartment and lighting it. This was the war which produced the 'Molotov Cocktail', a mixture of petrol or benzine, water and phosphorous with a piece of rubber added to make a sticky jelly with the benzine. The mixture was kept in bottles and just before throwing, it was shaken vigorously. On hitting a hard surface, the bottle smashed, the phosphorous ignited in the air and the benzine blazed merrily. A pint or so of burning petrol did not deter a tank very much, but in time the smoke was pulled into the crew compartment by the cooling fans, and the usual effect on the crew was to cause such alarm that they stopped and bailed out. In any case, the tanks of 1936 were all petrol-driven and the fuel tanks could be set alight if enough Molotovs were thrown. Molotovs are dangerous things both to carry and to throw, but the next weapon was even worse. This was a speciality of the Asturian miners of northern Spain.

They invented the satchel charge, which is simply a cloth bag filled with blasting explosives and fitted with a short-burning fuze and a pull switch. They attacked tanks by running up to them, pulling the fuze pin and throwing the charge either on to the engine deck or underneath the belly. The results were usually fatal for both tank and attacker, and the tanks soon learned to work in groups with each watching the other, but it also made them far more careful and less foolhardy. In fact so cautious did some become that the Spanish took advantage of it and used all sorts of simple ruses to deceive them. One, which became quite famous, occurred during a retreat when it became necessary to hold up some Italian light tanks which were pressing rather hard. A line was stretched across a village street a few feet off the ground and blankets were hung on to it so that they made a complete screen from one side to another. Two Italian light tanks appeared and stopped at the end of the street to fire their machine-guns through it. This had no effect, so one went back and brought up a medium tank. It fired several rounds from its gun, but refused to go through the screen; finally, after nearly half an hour, a shot cut the string, the screen fell down and the tanks gingerly felt their way forward. By this time the retreating Spaniards were well clear.

With war clouds gathering all over Europe, all countries looked to Spain to see what they could learn. Unfortunately most of the lessons were misleading, particularly those relating to the defeat of tanks. The trouble seems to have been that, whereas the designers of tanks and armoured vehicles saw very clearly that they had to improve armour and offensive gunnery, those whose speciality was the design of anti-armour weaponry were quite content with what they had, and took few active steps to improve anything. So it was that the 37mm guns stayed in service when they were only barely adequate, and anti-tank rifles (because they had not been tried) were assumed to be adequate and were ordered in quantity. There was apparently little co-operation between tank and anti-tank designers, otherwise the advances in tank protection might have sparked off some corresponding improvements in the weapons meant to overcome them.

In Britain the design team which had started work on an anti-tank rifle, acting on the inspiration of the Polish Marosczek, was headed by a Captain Boys. He unfortunately died a few days before the rifle passed its final tests and as a mark of respect, the team named the rifle after him. The original intention had been to call the rifle the Stanchion and the prototype still exists under that name. It was a bolt-action rifle which fed from a vertical box magazine much like the Bren gun. The barrel and receiver were carried on a slide and recoiled against the resistance of a powerful spring and there was also a large muzzle brake. Despite these precautions, the shock to the firer was considerable and unpleasant, as was the noise. It was the first British infantry weapon for which it was mandatory for the firer to wear ear plugs. Unlike the Polish rifle, the round was not steeply necked, and the calibre was 0·55in. The bullet was originally steel-cored but this was later found to be a mistake and tungsten carbide was substituted. The Boys was 5ft long and weighed 36lb, and for this bulk and weight, it would penetrate just over half an inch of armour at 300yd. The Army's anti-tank rifle training pamphlet for 1937 contains some charmingly optimistic advice. For instance, the instructor was urged to practise his squad in firing at a target representing a tank crossing his front at a range of 500yd and a speed of 15 to 25mph. Twenty mph is a good speed for a galloping horse and the reader might care to reflect for a moment on his chances of hitting a target moving at that rate, at a range of a quarter of a mile, even with a high-velocity rifle. The rewards for success should not be overlooked either. In the best case the tank would ignore the gadfly that was troubling it and go about its business; in the worst case it would get annoyed and come looking for its tormentor. Neither seems particularly profitable for the rifleman.

To supplement the Boys there was the 2-pounder gun. This was a beautifully made little weapon of great charm and precision. It had no trail in the accepted sense but folded down four outrigger legs which supported a central pivot and allowed a

360° traverse. The silhouette was rather high and the penetration rather feeble, but no objections were raised as it was well within the criteria for the Spanish Civil War and it was such a good example of the gun-founder's art that it won over the doubters without any difficulty. Unfortunately its very beauty told against it because it took an inordinate time to make and production never caught up with demand until it was too late.

Most of the countries which were to be involved on one side or the other in World War II were similarly equipped for anti-tank work. Nearly all had a gun of about 37mm, derived often enough from the 1916 Puteaux, and a large calibre of rifle to back it up. In Germany the gun was the PAK 36 and the rifle was the Pzb 38 (Panzerbuchse Model 1938), a beautifully made rifle of some complexity which resembled a small artillery piece in the way it used a sliding block to close the breech. The ammunition was a straight copy of the Marosczek and used the old Mauser 13mm case necked to a 7·92mm bullet with a tungsten-carbide core. The barrel and breech recoiled along a slide and opened the breech as it reached full travel, ejecting the empty case as it ran forward to battery. The gunner then pushed in another round by hand and the block snapped shut. Like the 2-pounder, it was so well made that one could not help being impressed; it was a pity that it was of so little value.

In France there was the 37mm, an improved Puteaux, but still not good enough for the tanks it would have to face. There was no rifle to fill in the gaps left by the gun although the French Army did have a few elderly 13·2mm AA machine-guns which could be used for anti-tank work. Poland had a Bofors 37mm and its Marosczek rifle, although this was by 1939 becoming danger-ously weak for the modern tanks. The Italians had a conventional 47mm gun, but only small numbers of it and no rifle or machine-gun at all. The US had a 37mm which was almost a complete copy of the German PAK 36. Two specimens of the first produc-tion batch of PAKs had been bought and tested in America and the results were sufficiently good to warrant copying it without, one is ashamed to report, too much respect for the niceties of patents or licensing arrangements. The US Army had been un-impressed with what it had seen of European anti-tank rifles

33

and preferred to pin its faith in the Browning 0·5in heavy machine-gun as a secondary infantry weapon. In Finland there was a departure from the norm, for in this tiny country and in this one alone had an anti-tank rifle of respectable size appeared. This was the Lahti, derived from an aircraft machine-gun of the same name. The Lahti was 20mm and could be fired either semi- or full automatic; it was gas-operated though the bolt is massive enough to make one believe that some use was also made of blow-back action. It was heavy, 95lb, and big, 88in long, but apparently an easy gun to fire owing to the usual elaborate recoil-reducing systems. One feature which emphasises the difficulties of fighting in Scandinavia is the bipod. The standard version has two sets of legs, one of which can be swung down and used, while the other is locked up against the barrel. One set of legs has normal spiked feet, but the other has a small ski on each foot; these would not only support the gun in the snow, but would also provide a firm base in the mud of the spring thaw. Also on the bipod attachment are two small spring-loaded equilibrators which help to overcome the difficulties of balancing a 95lb gun on two legs. How many of these superbly built guns took part in the 1939 Winter War is not known, but some at least played their part in holding off the Soviet armoured threat and perhaps helped the Russian Army to decide on its own policy towards infantry anti-armour weapons.

As the lights went out in Europe for the second time in a generation, and country after country lurched into war, each was quite confident that it had in service an adequate, if not a superior, anti-tank defence. Yet before a year had passed, each was to find how optimistic its predictions had been, how vulnerable its troops were, and how poorly the designers had prepared for the onset of an armoured war – a blitzkrieg.

(*Opposite*) Four anti-tank rifles of World War II:
A. The British Boys, introduced in 1938;
B. The German Pzb 39, introduced in 1940;
C. The German Grb 39, a cut-down Pzb fitted with a grenade-discharger cup on the shortened barrel;
D. The Soviet PTRS 41 semi-automatic rifle.

34

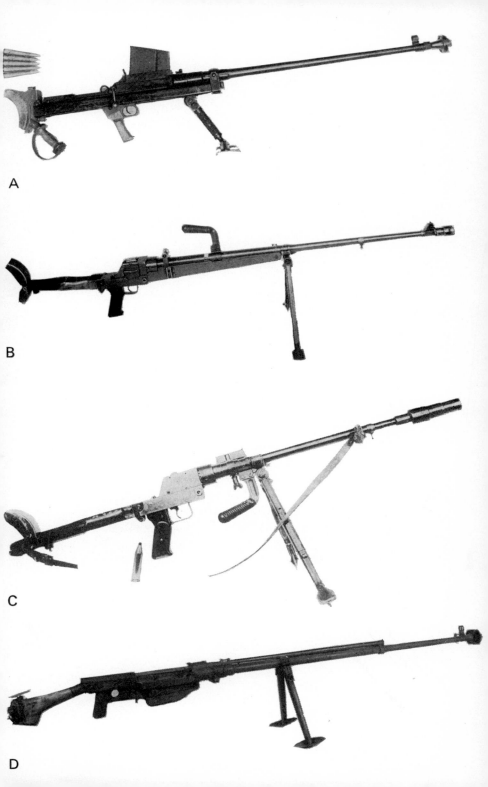

A

B

C

D

Page 36 (above) Direct hit! A jubilant German crew of a PAK 38 5cm anti-tank gun after knocking out two Soviet T-34s. A propaganda photograph from a wartime magazine; (below) A much-travelled anti-tank gun. A Soviet Model 1936 76·2mm field gun captured by the Germans and converted into an anti-tank gun. Shipped to North Africa, it was captured by the Allies in Tunis, 1943.

2
THE GREAT AWAKENING – BRITAIN, 1940

If the question is asked about any sort of tank, 'What is its weakest point?' the answer that should be given is always, 'The minds of the men inside it' . . .

Home Guard lecture, 1940

As the BEF sailed to France for the second time in a generation there were probably a few doubters who foresaw that if and when it came to a tank-to-infantry fight between the British and the Germans, the slender protection offered by the Boys and the 2-pounder was not going to be enough. But if these prophets existed in any numbers, they were wise enough to keep their opinions to themselves and the patriotic newspapers and magazines carried articles and photographs depicting the 'deadly new tank-killing guns' which were all too few in the units on the ground.

The blitzkrieg settled the doubts once and for all and the BEF returned via Dunkirk a much chastened army, short of equipment and with a greater respect for the tank as a battlefield weapon. To some extent the blitzkrieg reversed the German misfortunes of 1917; now it had been the turn of the British to be all but overwhelmed by tanks and the experience was most unpleasant. Because the army had to embark hurriedly – mainly across the Dunkirk beaches – no heavy equipment could be brought back and more than 500 2-pounders were left behind in France together with fifty or more Hotchkiss 25mm guns. The

C

latter were to some extent replaced by those that came back from the Norway campaign, but the total number of Hotchkiss guns in England was very small. They were either carried in 3-ton lorries or towed by ex-French Army Renault light tanks. It was soon found that it was better to mount the gun on top of its limber and tow that combination behind the tank since the wheels fell off the gun after a few miles of road work. With so few Hotchkiss guns, it was not worth setting up an ammunition production line, and when stocks were used up, the guns were scrapped.

Meanwhile the 2-pounder continued. This was a deliberate act of policy since the factories were tooled up for it and there was no other design available for mass production. Procrastination over the 6-pounder had ensured that it was still almost a year away, so the 2-pounder it had to be, despite misgivings about its effectiveness. The guns were issued as fast as they could be made and hurriedly set up in anti-invasion emplacements.

Moreover, work progressed on improvements to the 2-pounder. In December 1938 Dr F. Janecek, a Czech arms manufacturer, and his son Frantisek, became convinced that Germany would invade Czechoslovakia very soon. They had a new anti-tank gun design on the drawing boards of their small factory and were determined that it should not fall into German hands. Frantisek was sent to England and approached the Birmingham Small Arms Co who realised the importance of his ideas and put him to work in their Small Heath factory. In March 1939 the Germans invaded Czechoslovakia, but the night before they crossed the frontier, the British embassy was telephoned and a member of the staff went to the factory and took the prototype parts back to the embassy. Once in the embassy they were safe for the moment, but it took another three months to smuggle them out and into England, whence they went immediately to BSA. A few days before Britain declared war, a private car drove across Europe from Prague to the Channel ferry carrying the final drawings of the Janecek gun.

The gun which reached England in such dramatic fashion was a 'squeeze bore' attachment for the 2-pounder. Although the principle is very simple, the execution is more complicated and required much patient research and experiment to perfect it. In essence it was a short smooth-bored cone which was screwed on to the muzzle of the conventional barrel. It acted in much the same way as the Gerlich taper-bore guns. A special round was fired which was a slender tungsten-carbide cylinder with a soft metal 'band' or 'skirt' around its middle. This projectile went up the barrel in the normal way, the band sealing off the gas and gripping the rifling so that when it reached the muzzle of the original barrel, it was travelling at its usual muzzle-velocity and spinning. It now entered the additional cone-bore section, known incidentally as the 'Little John', and the metal band was steadily swaged down by the decreasing bore until it was no more than a thin coating when the projectile emerged and the majority of its mass had been smoothed into a lump at the rear of the tungsten carbide. The projectile left the Little John at a much higher speed than it would have done from the original muzzle, and this high speed, coupled with the mass of the tungsten carbide, gave it a better penetration and incidentally a flatter trajectory. By mid-1942 the Little John was in full production, but it never achieved the success the Janeceks had hoped for it and despite an attempt to fit Little Johns to 6- and 17-pounders, the idea was not pursued with much enthusiasm.

Several 2-pounder armoured cars were fitted with Little Johns in an effort to give them increased range and performance and a few appeared on infantry guns but in general the result was felt to be not worth the effort since tank armour had outstripped the device by the time it came into service. A few were retained on vehicles which could mount no other gun than the 2-pounder, and when the Airborne Reconnaissance Regiment flew into France in 1944 in its Hamilcar gliders, the Tetrach tanks still carried 2-pounders and most of these were fitted with Little Johns. By then they were not much more than an interesting anachronism.

The BEF did have one weapon, however, which gave them a lead over other armies. They were equipped with the world's first hollow-charge, anti-tank rifle grenade, in fact it was the first hollow-charge, anti-tank projectile of any kind and its story is almost as romantic as that of the Janeceks and the 2-pounder. At about the time of the 1938 Munich crisis, the British military attaché in Switzerland attended a demonstration of a new anti-tank explosive for which extravagant claims were made. A projectile was fired at a thick steel target and exploded on contact, leaving a small jagged hole right through the armour. The designers went to great lengths to conceal what they had done to achieve this effect, and demanded a steep price for the secret. The attaché was suspicious, not believing the designers' story that they had invented a new explosive of enormous power. He made a few investigations and discovered that they were using ordinary Nobels explosive bought on the commercial market and he immediately sent for an explosives expert to come from Woolwich to attend another demonstration. The designers were a little worried by this second demonstration and tried to lay a false scent by using dye in their explosive. However, the Woolwich man detected the secret quite quickly and identified it as an obscure laboratory phenomenon known as the Munro Effect – now well known as the Hollow Charge. The Swiss pair had hit upon a brilliant way of using the Munro Effect for a purpose that had never occurred to anyone before, that of punching a hole in armour plate and they must have cursed their luck that they had not closed the deal for less money in the first instance. As it was, they got nothing since they had invented nothing, and Britain began making a grenade that could be fired from the standard grenade-discharger cup fitted to the Short Magazine Lee Enfield rifle. A few trials confirmed its effectiveness and it was introduced into service as the No 68 grenade. The range from the rifle was only 100yd which made it somewhat of a last-ditch weapon, but even this was better than nothing.

The 68 grenade was declared obsolete before the war ended, partly because the cup discharger went out of favour, and partly because of improvements in the hollow-charge principle which meant that its $5\frac{1}{2}$oz of explosive could be used to better effect in other systems.

For Britain 1940 was a desperate time with the menace of an invasion by sea and air hanging over the country the whole summer. Within a few days of the end of Dunkirk, local civilians were organised into defence units and known as 'Parashots'. They stood guard over their villages and towns, armed with shotguns and filled with stories of Germans parachuting into battle disguised as nuns, parsons, or Allied soldiers. After about two weeks the Parashots were converted into Local Defence Volunteers or LDV who became the butt of many jokes. The LDV were given a slightly less aggressive role of observing and reporting, rather than actually tackling the invaders with their 12-bores. Very soon after the LDV was formed, there came yet another change and the Home Guard came into being in July 1940. The Home Guard was intended to be a para-military body with the primary task of defending the country against invasion. It started with hardly any equipment, few uniforms and little or no idea of how to fight tanks. They soon realised though that what they learned might sometimes lead them into serious difficulties had they tried to put it into practice against live tanks with trained crews.

The army was too busy retraining itself to be able to offer much help in the early stages when the urgency was greatest, and the Home Guard turned to the veterans of the Spanish Civil War for its instructors. The resulting doctrine placed an enormous premium on personal bravery for the only practical anti-tank weapons available to the Home Guard – and for many of the Regular Army for that matter – were grenades and explosives. A training centre was set up in Osterly Park just outside London and the creed of the Asturian miners was promulgated – together with some others of rather less value, for it was an unhappy fact that not all the instructors spoke with the same voice. No matter, the enthusiasm was there, and the students were keen enough. There was a feeling of destiny and drama in the air throughout the long summer of 1940 and more than one civilian volunteer wondered how long it would be until he had to fight from behind the walls of his own house.

A good deal of instructional effort was devoted to 'debunking' the invincibility of the tank and assuring the student that it was far less dangerous to be within 2yd of a tank than 200. Tanks, it was said, could be confused and frightened by the unknown or by the fear of imminent attack. The story of the Italian tanks in Spain and the blankets across the road was used frequently, as well as an account of a British company commander who in May 1940 gained a thirty-minute respite for his men while evacuating a French village under tank attack by laying five white soup plates upside down in the road. The German tanks, so the story went, refused to cross the soup plates in case they were mines and made a long detour which gave the company time to get clear. There were several similar stories and whether they were true or not is no longer important; they served their purpose at the time by reducing some of the terror of the armoured vehicle, but some of the advice was a little naive. For instance, in one lecture the class was told, 'Remember, men inside a tank can be worried by ·303 pinging on the outside or even shotgun blasts against the vision slits.' This seems an overstatement but the final sentence at the end of the class puts things back into perspective: 'Better to use any form of attack than nothing at all.'

There was much wishful thinking and misleading advice about stopping tanks. Whilst the light tanks of the Spanish Civil War might have been so low-powered that they could be brought to a stop by some sort of blockade, this was by no means certain for the German Panzers of 1940. The simplest idea was to hang a 2½in wire rope across a road, attaching the ends to trees; this, it was averred, would stop a tank by stalling its engine. No doubt, but 2½in wire rope is not easy to come by outside a naval dockyard, and is fiendish stuff to deal with. One wonders where the Spaniards found it in 1937. Another suggestion is quoted here in full because it gave rise to a complete legend in the Home Guard:

There is another way in which tanks can be stopped by brave men. Where the path that they will take comes close to thick cover, or consists of a narrow village street, you can wait for them with crowbars, lengths of tramline or similar metal. This is a job that is best done from the open doorway of a house against a tank travelling fairly slowly and very close to the house. The metal bar must be thrown or rammed into the side of the tank so that it gets in amongst the gear wheels and bogie wheels of the track. If a tank is travelling fast, the bar will probably be jerked from your hand and you will fail to get it in among the works. But if you can get it properly placed, the tank will be stopped and will probably block the road for those following it. For smaller tanks a pick slung into the tracks from the side will sometimes do the job.

Optimism was paramount in this method of attack, but it was later expanded into a proper drill using a team of four men, two holding the metal bar, one carrying a bucket of petrol, and the last one having either a Very pistol or fusee matches. As the tank passed, numbers one and two pushed the bar into the tracks to stop it; number three threw petrol on to the side, in some cases adding a blanket to soak up the petrol and keep it in one place; and number four came up and ignited the vehicle. The tank was then supposed to blaze merrily and the crew would be shot as they tried to get out.

Flame recurs frequently in the Home Guard manuals of this time, although Tom Wintringham was not enthusiastic about Molotov Cocktails saying that they were overrated and claiming that 10 per cent of the men using them ended up with serious burns. Others were of a different mind, and one pamphlet recommends their use in glowing terms, provided that the tank is less than 9 tons in weight, and then only if attacked from behind. This was the era of the home-made bomb and most of the Home Guard books go into great detail explaining how to make bombs suitable for defeating tanks. Wintringham recommended 2 or 3lb of explosive, which sounds right even today, but then went on to say that the fuze should be no longer than two or three seconds burning time, which gives the thrower no chance at all to get away.

Another speciality of the summer of 1940 was the most wonderful anti-tank grenade of them all, the Grenade, Hand, Anti-Tank No 74, or Sticky Bomb. So far there has never been another like it and most professional soldiers are content to keep it that way. The Sticky Bomb was a glass sphere containing 1¼lb of semi-liquid nitro-glycerine. A wooden handle contained a five-second fuze and the glass sphere was covered with stockingette material coated with a thick layer of bird-lime – hence the name. Over the whole sphere was a thin sheet-metal casing, made in two halves and held together at the handle. By pulling out a pin the casing could be dropped off leaving the sticky bird-lime exposed. The bomb was now ready for use. The technique was to get close to the target and throw the bomb with some force so that it struck the armour plate and broke the glass; the explosive then spread out into a 'cow pat' which was in close contact with the plate and when the fuze burnt down the explosion would penetrate armour less than 1in thick or severely damage thicker material. The fuze was set off by a lever which was released on throwing, but the bomb could also be placed on the target by hand, and this was recommended as being better than throwing. There were drawbacks to throwing. A careless swing could bring the bomb too close to the thrower and leave him trying to pry it loose from his clothing while striving to retain a hold on the lever; or the case might not break properly on impact, so the grenadier was urged to run up to his selected tank and smash the bomb on to the engine decking or the side. The Home Guard took to this terrifying device with some enthusiasm, but the Ordnance Board never approved it and in a publication in September 1940 said of it, 'The whole article is most objectionable!' It was never adopted for the Regular Forces, not that this stopped them using it in training exercises, and it was withdrawn in 1943 and decently buried. By that time the older versions were showing signs of deterioration in the nitro-glycerine, with the concomitant difficulties that arise from that state, so it was high time for it to go.

Another unpleasant grenade which first saw the light of day in 1940 was the Allbright and Wilson (AW) bomb, alias the Self Igniting Phosphorous Grenade (SIP), alias the Grenade, Hand, or Projector No 76. Messrs Allbright and Wilson were a firm of chemical engineers near Birmingham who were the principal producers of white phosphorous in the UK before the war and who invented the AW bomb as their contribution to the War Effort. It was a stubby glass bottle of roughly half-a-pint capacity, containing a fearsome mixture of white phosphorous, benzine, water and a piece of rubber which dissolved to make a sticky mess of the liquids, thus ensuring that they adhered to their target and did not just run off into the roadway. The bottle was closed by a crown cork. Red corks denoted throwing bombs; green ones were stronger bottles for firing from the Northover projector, of which more anon. The AW was issued only to the Home Guard and luckily was never used in battle. In effect it was the original Molotov Cocktail with improved ingredients, but it was highly dangerous to carry since it ignited the moment the glass bottle was broken or cracked, and the flames were not easily extinguished.

There were many others, all of them more or less dangerous to the user, and all requiring a high degree of dedication to be effective. What was urgently needed was some sort of gun or mortar for throwing these crude projectiles, and several Home Guard ballisticians made their own. Most of these were incredibly dangerous: the author has a clear recollection of a jam-tin bomb, thrown by 'private' mortar, landing in a nearby garden as a result of gross aiming error by the inventor, and the resulting explosion not only demolished a greenhouse, but was very nearly the cause of the Invasion Alert as well. The first proper Home Guard gun was the Northover projector. This was a simple smooth-bore gun with a barrel just less than 4ft long and a crude cast-iron breech block. Nominal calibre was $2\frac{1}{2}$in, but in fact it was $2\frac{5}{8}$in, just to make sure that nothing got stuck on its way to the muzzle. The barrel swung on four tubular legs which were dug into the ground and there was no recoil mechanism whatever. The sights were simple in the extreme, the rear sight being a bar pierced for ranges up to 200yd at 25yd intervals. The standard projectile was the AW bomb propelled by a cartridge containing black powder and several layers of thick rubber to avoid breaking the glass on firing. The black powder was ignited by a copper cap fitted externally on to a nipple in exactly the same way as with a Crimean musket; the flash penetrated the paper of the cartridge and ignited the powder. In the event of a misfire, the drill was to elevate the barrel and shake the bomb and cartridge down until both were closely in contact with the breech and then put on another cap and try again. Maximum range was 200yd, at which distance the AW bomb was turning over and over and the chance of hitting anything except by luck was remote. The Home Guard loved the beast and cheerfully carried its 74lb around with them. It was their artillery.

Soon after the Northover the Home Guard were given another anti-tank weapon; this was the Blacker Bombard or 29mm spigot mortar. Lt-Colonel Blacker was a prolific inventor of low-cost weapons and the Bombard was his awesome answer to the tank. It was a large spigot mortar which fired a 20lb anti-tank bomb to a range of a few hundred yards, although the best fighting range was 150. The mortar was enormously heavy, 405lb, so that for the most part, it was used as an emplacement weapon in prepared ambush positions with adequate cover. The bomb was fired at 245ft per second which meant that it took more than one and a half seconds to reach 150 yards, and for moving targets, a shorter range was desirable. However, it was quite accurate and the bomb was enormously destructive, well capable of blowing the turret off a Mark I or II if it hit it in the right place. The crew was four men and a commander, and more were needed if the mortar was to be moved. Although not a very practical weapon, the Bombard was something and it would probably have given a good account of itself if it had to be used in anger. Perhaps it is as well for the crews that it never was. The 1941 training pamphlet has one interesting paragraph which no longer is found in military publications. In it are the actions to be taken if the Bombard has to be abandoned and capture is inevitable; most of the measures are concerned with the bending of vital parts, but if recapture appears possible, then a less stringent form of destruction was advocated.

Another 1940 special was the Smith gun, the child of the fertile brain of a military gentleman of that name. In effect, it was a smooth-bore gun on wheels and was not much more effective than the Northover though it was far more complicated and heavy. The carriage was a pair of dished steel discs, shod with thin high-pressure pneumatic tyres. The barrel pivoted on the axle, but to fire, the Smith gun was deployed in a manner unique in the history of artillery, for it was turned on its side and the axle became vertical and one wheel became the base on which the gun roated. The other wheel then gave some limited overhead cover, though not much more than would keep out the rain. Ammunition came in a limber of the same pattern as the gun, though it was left standing on its two wheels at the gun site and not tipped up. Ammunition was the standard range for 1940, grenades, petrol bombs, and a small HE bomb. Effective range was about 250yd and armour penetration low. Not many were made and all were exclusively a Home Guard issue – the Regular Army wouldn't touch it.

Finally there was flame. Although petrol stocks were not large in 1940, there was far more petroleum than there was explosive or guns and several minds bent themselves to the task of determining how best to use fire as a deterrent to armoured vehicles. The best and simplest way was not to try to ignite the tank because it was known that that was difficult – despite what the Home Guard were being taught – it was better to surround the vehicle with a sea of fire and literally starve it of oxygen. Oxygen for the engine and oxygen for the crew were both needed in large quantities and a big enough fire would use up all that was in and around the tank. It took less than six seconds to stop a 1940 tank through oxygen starvation and the planning was based on this figure. Obviously it was difficult to provide for mobile flame projectors that could throw as much fuel as would be needed for six seconds of burning time, so most of the devices were static and intended to be pure ambush weapons. In the main there were four types:

    Static Flame Traps
    Flame Fougasses, Demi-Gasses and Hedge-Hoppers
    Beach Flame Barrages
    Home Guard Flame Throwers

The Static Flame Traps were self-explanatory. They were some system of projecting fuel on to a road or track and igniting it. Most of them consisted of large drums of fuel dug into hillsides about 200ft from the track with pipes leading to the verges. Nearly all were gravity fed, but there were a few which needed pumps to force the fuel to the jets. The fuel was 25 per cent petrol and 75 per cent gas oil. Ignition was by using a Very pistol or a Molotov Cocktail, and to cover 60ft of road 30 gallons of fuel was needed every minute. By June 1941 there were 168 of these traps up and down the length of Britain, some of which had enough fuel for twenty minutes burning.

Fougasses were a variation on the flame trap in which the fuel was projected by explosive. A Fougasse was generally made by burying a 40-gallon oil drum into a road bank and installing a pound or two of guncotton behind it, together with some incendiary mixture. On firing, a sheet of flame 10ft wide and 30yd long was fired across the road. A Demi-Gasse was the same as a Fougasse but was sited in the open without the advantage of the cover of the bank. On firing the barrel was blown apart and flame spread for an area of 36sq yd. It was less efficient than the proper

47

Fougasse, but useful in confined spaces. The Hedge-Hopper was a barrel standing on end with a charge placed off-centre beneath it. When fired, the barrel jumped 10ft into the air and travelled 7yd horizontally, flooding its landing area with blazing fuel.

These unpleasant devices would obviously not work well against moving tanks and for success it was intended that the enemy vehicles would have to be halted by other means, such as the famous soup plates in the road, or a mine in the tracks of the leader, or a barrier of some sort. The Fougasse would then be sprung and before the hapless enemy could back away, the fatal six seconds would have elapsed and the engines would stop. Whether it would always have worked so well is highly problematical, but the psychological impact of sheets of flame pouring around the tank would probably have been good enough. By June 1941 when the invasion scare was dying down, there were over 7,000 flame-trap sites of one kind or another set up and in working order all over Britain and there were more than 12,000 barrels in them. Another 27,000 extra barrels were on order.

Beach Flame Barrages started with the idea that an invasion could be stopped by pouring liquid fuel on to the sea and igniting it as the landing craft approached the beach. It was shown that a mixture of petrol, kerosene and oil could be pumped out to some yards from the shore in undersea pipes and ignited using calcium phosphide; but waves, wind and currents made it impossible to achieve a consistent effect and the idea was abandoned in favour of flame barrages on the foreshore and exit points from landing area. More than fifty miles of these beach barrages were erected, all with the sole intention of destroying armoured vehicles as they left their shipping. Wartime rumour persistently circulated a story that the German Army tried an invasion in late 1940 and that all the boats and men were burned to a cinder by a vast sheet of flame poured on to the sea. There were even some who averred that charred bodies were washed up on the south coast, but it was all wishful thinking possibly inspired by gossip after one of the trials with the early type of Beach Barrage. The flame weapons were never put to the test, and in the latter days of the war Royal Engineer demolition parties had the tricky job of dismantling them and draining off their rusted containers. The feed pipes were often left in the ground and were still being pulled out twenty years later.

In fact until very recently England abounded in relics of the invasion scare of 1940. In some less frequented rural areas it is still possible to find the concrete roadblocks standing in the hedgerows. Most of these were made by filling 40-gallon oil drums with concrete and putting a pipe down the middle. A pole could then be shoved into the hole and the cylinder of concrete manhandled into the road. Eight or ten were needed for an effective block but all too many were sited so that it was no trouble at all for a tank to pick another route and go around the obstacle. An exception existed until recently near the author's home where the approaches to a railway bridge had been prepared for blocking by inserting rather elaborate square holes into the road and covering each one with its own individual iron lid. When the invasion alarm was sounded, the lids were taken off and lengths of railway line stood upright in them, thereby making an effective and strong fence which few 1940 tanks would have been able to do much about. There was no alternative way round as the railway runs in a cutting at this point, and the bridge was covered by a concrete pill box cleverly sited on the other side of the bridge. This is in northern Wiltshire – a long way from the beaches.

The fourth and final flame weapon was the Home Guard Flame Thrower. This was not quite what its name might lead one to believe. It was both crude, simple and probably dangerous; it was made with the available stores by the Petroleum Warfare Department and issued by them direct to Home Guard units. It consisted of a 65-gallon barrel containing a 40/60 petrol/diesel mixture, a semi-rotary hand pump, and 100ft of hose all mounted on a two-wheeled barrow or trolley. It was designed to be used for the static defence of a strong point or a road block and its mobility was limited to a movement of a few yards pulled or pushed by its team of four or five Home Guard operators. The range was about 15yd and the flame could be kept going for two minutes or so. In use the jet at the end of the hose was connected to a stand pipe or similar support and ignition was by lighting a piece of oily rag or by throwing an Allbright and Wilson bomb. It was a clumsy and inefficient weapon which could only be justified by the urgent need to give the Home Guard something with which to meet the expected armoured invasion. Only 250 were issued and these were withdrawn by the end of 1942.

As the warm summer of 1940 faded into the mists and winds of the autumn equinox the British heaved a sigh of relief for it was obvious to all that there was no danger of invasion now until the following spring and there was time to improve the hurried and ineffective defences which had sufficed for the past months. As this was being done the focus of attention moved away from the southern beaches of England to more distant and warmer climates. The first rumblings of the Desert War were making themselves heard.

3
THE WEHRMACHT

Germany is proud of her Panzer divisions, and I am happy to be your commander!

General Guderian, May 1940

Germany started World War II with a very similar anti-tank armoury to that of her opponents. The basis was the light towed gun, PAK 35/36 of 37mm, and a fairly wide issue of anti-tank rifles to the infantry. Within the infantry battalion the only anti-tank weapon was the rifle, which was issued on a basis of three per infantry company. The 37mm guns were held in a special anti-tank company of which there was one allocated to each infantry regiment. Confidence in this gun was confirmed in the Polish campaign in August and September of 1939, although the Polish armour equipments were so limited in their effectiveness that it was by nowhere near a fair test, and this was amply brought out in the next year when the gun came up against the heavily armoured British tanks in France.

The efficiency of the PAK 35/36 really rested on its mobility. It was a light gun, weighing 8½cwt and running on two large wheels with pneumatic tyres. The crew could manhandle it with very little difficulty; it could be towed by a car or some similar light vehicle; and was little trouble to put into the back of a lorry or on to a railway flatcar. It had obvious attractions for the newly formed airborne units of the Luftwaffe and for mountain troops. It fired both armour-piercing and HE ammunition and so could be used in a variety of tasks and not just confined to the simple one of attacking armoured vehicles. Its Achilles' Heel lay in its ability to penetrate armour, or rather in its comparative inability to penetrate armour. What had seemed to be a satisfactory standard in 1934 was well out of date by 1939, but this had been concealed by the obsolescence of the tanks in Spain and Poland, and the small shell of the PAK was easily defeated by sloped armour plate.

When the blitzkrieg burst upon France in 1940 the PAK 35/36 went with the armoured forces as the backbone of the anti-tank defence. It proved not to live up to its expectations as this account by Brigadier Douglas Pratt in *The Tanks* by Basil Liddell-Hart tells; he is relating the events of 20 May 1940 near Arras:

> During this time we played hell with a lot of Boche motor transport and their kindred stuff. Tracer ammunition put up a lot in flames. His anti-tank gunners after firing a bit, bolted and left their guns, even when fired at from ranges of 600 to 800 yards with machine guns from Matildas. Some surrendered and others feigned dead on the ground! None of his anti-tank stuff penetrated our Is and IIs and not even did his field artillery which fired high explosive. Some tracks were broken and a few tanks were put on fire by his tracer bullets, chiefly in the engine compartment of the Matilda Is. One Matilda had fourteen direct hits from one of his 37mm guns and it had no harmful effect, just gouged out a bit of armour!
>
> The main opposition came from his field guns, some of which fired over open sights. Also the air dive bombing on the infantry – this of course did not worry the tanks much. One or two bombs bursting alongside a Matilda turned it over and killed the commander; another lifted a light tank about fifteen feet in the air!

The German commander in this action was Major-General Rommel and his account confirms the inadequacy of the 37mm gun:

> The anti-tank guns which we quickly deployed showed themselves to be far too light to be effective against the heavily armoured British tanks, and the majority of them were put out of action by gunfire, together with their crews, and then over-run by the enemy tanks. Many of our vehicles were burnt out. S.S. units close by also had to fall back to the south before the weight of the tank attack. Finally the divisional artillery and the 88mm anti-aircraft batteries succeeded in bringing the enemy armour to a halt south of the line Beaurains-Agny. Twenty-eight enemy tanks were destroyed by the artillery alone, while the anti-aircraft guns accounted for one heavy and seven light.

The success of the anti-aircraft guns was not lost on Rommel who employed the 88s to even better effect two years later in the Western Desert.

Page 53 (*above*) The German 88mm PAK 43, the Krupp gun which became the terror of the Allied armour. This specimen is in the gun park of the Aberdeen Proving Ground today, and the picture brings out the considerable height of the whole equipment above the ground; (*below*) The Junkers 87 fitted with two semi-automatic 37mm AA guns for anti-tank duties. On the gun nearest to the camera can be seen the box magazine sticking out to the side.

Page 54 (above) The British infantry anti-tank weapon of World War II, the PIAT. A short-range spigot mortar of unusual design, it stayed in service until about 1949; (below) A US M1 57mm anti-tank gun firing on a Japanese position on the island of Luzon, Philippines, in 1945. The M1 was almost identical with the British 6-pounder from which it was derived.

The campaign in France proved beyond doubt that the 37mm guns were no good any longer and work was put in hand immediately to bring on the next designs, which at this time were in existence but not yet ready for production. Meanwhile, the 37mm would have to suffice and to give it another lease of life a better anti-tank round was produced with a higher muzzle-velocity and about 30 per cent better penetration. Until the next generation came along, that had to do. Luckily for the Wehrmacht, there was a comparative lull in armoured warfare in late 1940 and early 1941 and the deficiencies of the 37mm were glossed over.

The companion weapon to the gun had been the infantry anti-tank rifle the Pzb 38, or Panzerbuchse, Model 1938. The action of this unusual rifle has already been described, and it was popular with the infantry who used it. At least, one should qualify that by saying that it was popular until its ineffectiveness was shown up. As with so many German equipments, it bristled with novelties, most of which were good and were a help to the gunner. However, things got a bit out of hand with the ammunition. The bullet had a tungsten-carbide core, at the base was a tracer element, and between that and the tungsten carbide, marvellous to relate, was a small pellet of tear gas! The tungsten core was a sensible and useful way of ensuring that the bullet had the best possible penetrative ability. The tear-gas pellet was an extraordinary waste of effort. The idea was that when the bullet entered the tank, the pellet would be crushed and a cloud of gas released which would, presumably, reduce the surviving crew members to helpless snuffling and blindness. Since the pellet was hardly any bigger than an aspirin, the size of the cloud was not likely to be noticed at all. Nor was it; it was only when captured ammunition was broken down that it was discovered.

However, notwithstanding the mouse-sized gas attack, the Pzb 38 did well in Poland and so there was made another dangerous reputation because, as with the 37mm gun, the blitzkrieg soon showed that this rifle did not have the penetrating power to be of much use. But there was nothing else, and a simpler version of it called the Pzb 39 was put into production and issued in late 1940 and early 1941 on a fairly wide scale. The Pzb 39 did away with the recoiling barrel and the automatic opening of the breech –

this was now done by the gunner pushing down his pistol grip – which meant a gun weighing 7lb less while retaining the same performance. Their best penetration was just over one inch of armour plate at 100yd, and at 300 about ¾in of plate could be defeated. It was enough for armoured cars or the back and sides of some light tanks, but useless for head-on attackers.

By late 1940 the first examples of a new anti-tank gun appeared. This was a scaling-up progression of the 37mm and it was tied to the family of main armament guns for the German tanks. By using the same calibre in both tanks and anti-tank guns, there were substantial savings to be made in production and from 1940 onwards, one type of projectile was common on both types of gun. It was not always possible to have the same barrel for both, nor even the same breech, but great efforts were made to keep the two as alike as possible. This new gun was the PAK 38 and it was destined to be the mainstay of the anti-tank armoury for the rest of the war. It was a comparatively light gun, just about one ton, for its size, and had an effective muzzle brake to reduce the recoil of the barrel. This in turn allowed for a lighter recuperator mechanism and so a lower overall weight. The wheels were shod with solid rubber tyres to reduce maintenance and use of rubber, already scarce; the road shocks were taken up by a supple and strong torsion-bar suspension. These two features, the muzzle brake and torsion-bar suspension, were immensely successful and were employed on every subsequent design of German anti-tank gun that was produced. The designs were already on the drawing boards before the first PAK 38 was issued and work was going ahead feverishly, some of it to meet military specifications and some of it along novel lines laid down by the designers themselves.

The unorthodox designers were first in the field with what has been described as the only really 'secret weapon' of the war. These were the first coned-bore guns and their existence was never suspected until they were met in battle. The principle was not novel – it had been known since the early years of the twentieth century – and attempts had been made to use it in sporting as well as military rifles. None of these had succeeded, but now a German designer named Gerlich applied it to an anti-tank gun. Gerlich's version was a gun with a bore which tapered uniformly from

28mm at the breech to 20mm at the muzzle. At the same time the rifling increased its rate of twist so that as the projectile speeded up in the barrel, it also spun faster and so remained stable in flight. There were of course formidable difficulties in making such a gun, particularly in machining a tapered barrel, but the increase in muzzle-velocity was so dramatic that it seemed worthwhile. The 20mm projectile with a tungsten-carbide core was fired out from the muzzle at very nearly 4,600ft per second, which was an unheard of speed in 1941. Penetration was good up to 800yd, although it fell off after that distance. The equipment was incredibly light for what it did – just over 500lb – and an airborne version was made with a flimsy-looking tubular carriage which turned the scales at 260lb.

But there was a price to be paid for all this. Firstly, it was in the performance; although described as 'good', it was only good for a gun of that size; in hard fact the penetration was only a little bit better than the obsolescent PAK 35/36 and this was not really offset by the weight saving. The other part of the price was in the ammunition. The projectile was in effect a 20mm shot with a soft alloy sheath around it and two soft circular 'skirts' which fitted the starting calibre. On firing, the skirts filled the barrel and made a gas-tight seal, but were smoothed down by the decreasing bore and the emerging projectile was a long 20mm slug, with a heavy tungsten core up at the front. To make this ammunition required more than the average amount of machining time and skill and there was the concomitant disadvantage that the core had to be of tungsten carbide and the supply of this material became so critical that none could be spared for anti-tank work. There were other drawbacks also. Only armour-piercing rounds could be fired from this taper-bore gun, there was no capability to shoot HE shell, and the life of the barrel was limited to about 500 rounds. After that it was worn out, particularly at the muzzle where the strain was greatest.

So the 28/20mm guns (designated 2·8cm S Pzb 41) were made only in small numbers. They were beautifully constructed weapons with the then novel arrangement of a free traverse which allowed the gunner to swing the gun in azimuth and elevation by simply pushing the handgrips instead of having to turn

57

handwheels. Although not used in any appreciable numbers, the 28/20 started a fashion which was followed by several others.

The next one was the 42/30, or 4·2cm 1e PAK 41 which as the name implies fired a round which tapered from 42mm at the breech to 30mm at the muzzle. This again was only produced in small numbers, but it did try to overcome one of the objections to taper-bore weapons by offering an HE shell, but it only weighed 10oz and can have hardly been of much use. The gun used the same carriage as the 37mm PAK 35/36 and like the 28/20 guns was intended to be controlled and fired by one gunner.

By the autumn of 1941 the 50mm PAK 38 guns were appearing in substantial numbers in the Western Desert where the anti-tank defence had until then relied on the 37mm. The German gunners soon realised the value of the new gun and began to use it in the attack as well as defence. This was a new trick to the British who took time to find an answer to it, and, until they did, they had to give way as this extract from Heinz Schmidt's book *With Rommel in the Desert* shows:

> ... We had now developed a new method of attack. With our twelve anti-tank guns we leap-frogged from one vantage point to another, while our Panzers, stationary and hull down if possible, provided protective fire. Then we would establish ourselves to give them protective fire while they swept on again ... The tactics worked well, and despite the liveliness of his fire the enemy was not able to hold up our advance. He steadily sustained losses and had to give ground constantly ...

The PAK 38 could knock a hole through 2in of armour at a thousand yards if it hit at a 30° slope, and much more than that at right angles. The silhouette of the gun was very low indeed and if a gun pit little more than 2ft deep was dug, the barrel came down nearly to the ground so that the emplacement all but disappeared.

To give the infantry something more useful than the clumsy but ineffective anti-tank rifles an attempt was made to turn the Pzb 39 into a grenade-thrower. The barrel was cut down and a launcher tube screwed on to the muzzle. This launcher took the same types of grenades as the standard infantry rifle and fired them to about the same range, that is 200yd maximum. The anti-tank rifle was supposed to shoot them more accurately owing to its greater weight and the use of a bipod. It was not a very happy modification and can hardly have been greeted with much joy by the infantry since the grenades had roughly the same poor performance as the original armour-piercing bullet yet their range was shorter.

Another modification to an existing weapon was to turn the PAK 35/36 gun into a grenade-launcher also. The bomb that it fired was perhaps a little large to be called a grenade since it weighed 19lb and was 30in long, but it looked exactly like many other muzzle-launched grenades that were fired from rifles and it had about the same range. The tail boom on this bomb was hollow and fitted over the muzzle of the gun, and the fins were attached to this boom. Inside the boom was a solid rod which fitted into the bore and acted as the gas check for the propellant. The bulbous nose of the bomb held 5lb of explosive arranged as a 'hollow charge' and it would blow a hole in 5in of armour plate. A type of blank cartridge was used to fire the bomb, and it must have been fairly inaccurate at any range greater than 200yd because of the fact that it had virtually no barrel length to give it direction. Another drawback was that, to reload, one member of the crew had to go round to the front of the gun and slide another bomb on to the muzzle, so the chances of a second shot were just about nil. It must have taken uncommonly brave men to use it.

However, by the end of 1941 the Wehrmacht was finding that it needed a large number of uncommonly brave men if it was to survive at all. The drive into Russia had gone well for the first few months but with the fall of winter the Russians were showing signs of counter-attacking, and attacking with large numbers of tanks – good tanks at that. Some of these were KV 1s, slow, very heavy, not well armed but so heavily protected as to be almost impervious to any gun except an 88mm Flak. For various reasons the KV 1 did not last long, nor were there ever very many of them, but the ones that the Germans did meet gave them a most unpleasant surprise.

The first encounter came in Lithuania where a KV 1 interposed itself between a German bridgehead over a river and the remainder of the force some miles back down the road. The tank simply stood still in the middle of the road, and when the Germans brought up a battery of six PAK 38 guns, their shells bounced off the armour. The tank then traversed its 76·2mm gun and at a range of 900yd knocked out two of the guns, damaged all the others and caused severe casualties to the crews, whilst remaining apparently unharmed. That night twelve German engineers crawled up to the KV 1 and put satchel charges under the suspension. These failed to cut the tracks or cause any obvious damage and the engineers were lucky to get away with their lives. The next day an 88mm Flak gun from the bridgehead worked its way slowly towards the stationary KV 1 and positioned itself about 800yd from it, seemingly without being seen. Just as the 88's crew were putting the finishing touches to their position, the Russian tank swung its gun around and blew the 88 into the ditch. The situation was becoming serious: one tank was holding up an entire divisional advance.

Next day six German tanks manoeuvred in the woods and fired on the KV 1 from different directions at the same time. Their shells did no harm, but the Russian kept up a continual return fire and failed to notice another 88mm Flak gun that was pulled into a position behind it. This gun finally knocked out the KV 1, firing seven shots to do it. Even then the crew was still alive and had to be killed with hand-grenades thrown through the loosened ports. On examining the Russian tank, the German gunners were a little shaken to find that only two of the 88's shells had penetrated, the others leaving only deep dents in the plating. The 50mm shells from the tanks had done no more than make blue marks. Much sobered, the German division moved on, having been held up for forty-eight hours by one tank.

The Russian T-34s were quite impervious to the PAK 35/36 which was all that the companies had, and the anti-tank rifles were so useless that the troops simply left them behind as they moved up to the front. The only really effective way to knock out a Russian tank was to get so close to it that it was possible to throw a large explosive charge on to the rear decking, or to drop a Teller mine under the tracks, or to throw a fuzed Teller mine under the overhang of the turret. These were desperate measures and the losses in infantry who tried them were very high, but there was no other way until some better guns could be issued and these were some way off. Some brave men remained in their trenches until the T-34s were only a few yards away and then stood up and fired their rifle grenades into the side or rear armour. Sometimes it worked; all too often it didn't and an infuriated tank turned round and destroyed the infantryman.

One expedient which was quite successful was a revival of a method of attack developed in World War I. Five or six stick grenades were made into one charge, and the fuze from one was used to set off the entire bundle. The resulting explosion was enough to penetrate the engine deck of a T-34 and stop the engine, but it took a brave and determined man to do it. Another expedient was to try and adapt as many weapons as possible to fire some sort of hollow-charge grenade. Even the signal pistol was found to have enough power to shoot the smallest of the rifle grenades, weighing just over 4oz, and a special egg grenade which was made for the pistol which carried a larger – but still inadequate – bursting charge. Whether any tanks were ever damaged by these tiny projectiles is highly problematical, and how many brave men were needlessly killed trying to shoot them at Russian tanks will never be known either. It seems most unlikely that the troops can have had any faith in such obvious toys.

In the search for a quick solution yet another anti-tank rifle was tried. This was the biggest and best of all the German family and, had it appeared two years before, might have had a chance to make a name for itself. In 1941 it was too late by a long way. It was the Panzerbuchse 41, a beautifully and expensively made 20mm semi-automatic, clip-fed, air-cooled, anti-tank rifle. It originated in a Solothurn design of 1933 which was modernised by the team of Herlach and Rakula in 1938. Even at that date, it was realised that 7·92mm bullets were already inadequate and what was needed was greater momentum and energy. Herlach and Rakula took the largest practical size of ammunition for a single man to fire and put the improved Solothurn around it. The gun was made by Rheinmetall and is sometimes known by their name and sometimes as the Solothurn.

A quick-change barrel was locked by a fermeture nut to the bolt and the whole was designed to fire while the working parts were still going forward. This meant that the recoil had to overcome the momentum of the combined mass of the barrel and bolt before pushing the mechanism backwards and this made for such a gentle recoil at the firer's shoulder that US Army test firers claimed that it was no worse than that from an '03 Springfield rifle. Cocking was done by turning a crank handle on the right-hand side which wound up a bicycle chain and pulled the working parts to the rear. Once that was done, successive shots would re-cock the action. The magazine fed in from the left-hand side and held five rounds. The all-up weight of the infantry version, including the bipod, was a staggering 97lb. A crew of two or three was essential and for this expenditure of manpower one achieved a penetration of 30mm or $1\frac{1}{4}$in of armour at a range of 250yd. Although this was twice as good as the other rifles, it was absolutely hopeless for the medium tanks of 1941 and 1942. Already the 37mm shells of the PAK 35/36 bounced off the sides of the T-34 so a 20mm, no matter how fast it went, would be no better. There were other drawbacks also. The mechanism was complicated and demanded intricate machining to manufacture. The gun was sensitive to dirt and snow and tiring to move. Because of its two- or three-man firing team, it was of little use in the rifle company, which was where it was needed and the one place where its performance, poor though it was, could best be utilised. As it was, it became a special battalion weapon and, although popular with some troops, was never used in large numbers. Many were handed to the Italian Army who used it in North Africa and Sicily, and still had it in the inventory at the surrender in 1943.

These expedients did little to help the front-line infantry who were now finding the Russian tank attacks becoming more and more formidable and the outlook for 1942, in so far as anti-tank guns went, looked bleak for the Germans, despite their territorial gains. Fortunately there was some relief to be had. The first was the PAK 40, a 7·5cm gun of native design. Contracts had been placed for such a gun in 1939 with both Krupp and Rheinmetall-Borsig but due to the pressures of other work, neither was ready for production by the start of the Russian campaign. As soon as the limitations of the existing equipments were seen, the PAK 40 contracts were speeded up.

Rheinmetall-Borsig, alive to the heavy demands on factory effort in wartime, had produced a standard parallel-bore gun which was similar in design to the existing 5·ocm PAK 38 which was being so successful. The Krupp version was known as the PAK 41 to distinguish it from the other gun and was another taper-bore design. The PAK 40 won the contract on the grounds of simplicity and familiarity and went into full-scale production. It was used with considerable success throughout the rest of the war and its penetration performance of 94mm (3·7in)/at 30° at 1,000m was considered to be entirely satisfactory. Later on there were second thoughts in some quarters because simplicity has to be paid for somehow and the gun was heavier than its crew could easily manage (it weighed 1 ton 9cwt, or 3,300lb) and in the spring thaws and winter mud in Russia, many perfectly serviceable guns had to be abandoned because their crews could not haul them out of their positions to where a tractor could get to them.

Although the PAK 41 lost the contract, it still went into limited production as part of a German policy of hedging one's bets. About 150 were made and were issued to special duty regiments who had them until the supply of ammunition dried up. The PAK 41 had several novel features. The barrel was in two parts, the breech half being an ordinary parallel-bored gun with rifling. The forward half was a smooth-bored squeeze tube which narrowed the projectile down to an emergent calibre of 55mm, the ammunition being of course the usual skirted type with a tungsten-carbide core. This projectile brought about the downfall of the gun because the supplies of tungsten were so small that after 1941 all ammunition which required it ceased to be made. This was in many ways a pity because the gun was very good and might even have been chosen before the Rheinmetall design, had it not been for the tungsten position. The penetration was about 50 per cent better than the PAK 40 and the gun was lighter by some 300lb and featured an exceptionally well-designed carriage which was both low and light. The shield of this carriage was a structural member and supported both the barrel and the trail legs. The barrel itself was slung in a ball mounting in front of the shield and was very easily traversed and elevated. The front half of the barrel had a life of 500 rounds and could be unscrewed and changed in the field by the crew. When all were worn out and the special ammunition had been fired off, some of these guns were fitted with the barrel from their rival, the PAK 40, and were continued in service.

But it was not the new designs which saved the day for the Wehrmacht in the difficult days of 1942. The stopgap which saw it through until the new models could be made in sufficient numbers was a Russian gun, or rather two Russian guns. The one which did most of the work was the Russian 76·2mm Field Gun Model 1936. Very large numbers of these were captured in the first offensives in 1941 and they were quickly modified and given a better carriage and put straight back into use as anti-tank guns. Their performance was not brilliant but it was adequate and with an improved German-designed shell and larger chamber capacity, it became a reliable and well-liked workhorse. Its drawback was once again, weight. It was 400lb heavier than the PAK 40 and so that much harder to manhandle. Another Russian gun which was turned against its original owners was the Model 1939 Field Gun which was simply an improved version of the 1936 model. Both of these Russian guns were backed up by a modified version of the venerable French Model 97 75mm Field Gun. The modifications were fairly far-reaching and involved a new carriage, trail and shield together with a 'pepper-pot' muzzle brake so that the original nationality did not become apparent until the breech was examined, and there was the old Nordenfelt screw. The German crews were not happy with these 75mm guns, chiefly because they were unstable and too high to conceal easily, but whatever their failings, they helped the Wehrmacht to get over a bad patch and were then relegated to the reserve to await the closing days of the war when a few would be pulled out from store and put into action once again.

By 1943 two aspects of the anti-tank war had become clearly apparent to the Wehrmacht. The first was that the infantry simply had to have some effective means of knocking out enemy tanks even if the range of the means was quite short. It was useless to go on sacrificing men in futile grenade and explosive attacks. The Russians now carried infantry on their tanks, known as Tank Riders, to give them protection against this menace; while on the other fronts, the desert battles were over and another much more difficult infantry war was looming up in Italy.

Fortunately for the Germans, there was a quick solution near at hand. A shipload of the first model American Bazookas had been sent to Russia in 1942 and the Germans captured some soon after. The advantages of the rocket projector were seen immediately and within seven or eight months, an improved German version was being issued to troops in Russia. This projector, the 8·8cm Racketenpanzerbuchse was much bigger than the Bazooka and fired a bomb twice the size. The principle was exactly the same, and the fighting range was also the same, that is about 100yd, but the penetration of the bomb was better. The RacketenPzb was popular with the troops and effective against the T-34 which encouraged the designers to try to improve it still further by increasing the calibre to 100mm. It was a failure. The weight of the launcher went up to nearly 30lb and it became inordinately long and unwieldy. The increase in range and performance was not so great as to justify the extra bulk and the idea died. But the 8·8cm version was ideal and it remained in service in large numbers on all fronts until the end of the war.

The second aspect was that, despite the advances in anti-tank guns and the 7·5cm PAK 40s which were being issued in reasonably large numbers, there were still some enemy tanks which needed to be knocked out beyond the ranges that these guns could reach; so yet another design was required. Although there were several designs in preparation, the obvious one to choose was one which had already showed itself to be entirely reliable and successful, namely the Flak 88. Luckily a requirement had been put out in 1940 for a dual-purpose 88mm anti-tank AA gun and by late 1942 both Krupp and Rheinmetall-Borsig had pilot models ready. The Rheinmetall gun was much more of an AA gun than an anti-tank so it went into production as the 8·8cm Flak 41. The Krupp gun on the other hand was an anti-tank gun first and an AA gun second, so it became the 8·8cm PAK 43 even though it was mounted on a light version of the four-legged AA platform. Despite the apparent size and complexity of this platform the gun was easily handled, yet in the firing position it was unnaturally high off the ground. As production got under way, the barrel-makers outstripped the carriage-makers, a phenomenon not altogether unknown in weapon production, and some other carriages had to be found. A hurried hybrid two-wheeled carriage was put together using parts from 105mm howitzer manufacture, and although not a perfect result, it did mean that guns could be put into action at a time when they were desperately needed. This gun was known as the PAK 43/41 and was rather high, awkward, and unstable; but it held the gap until the better PAK 43 appeared in sufficient numbers.

The 88mm series of guns remained in front-line service for the remainder of the war with no real challengers competing against them. But to move them was difficult enough. In the desert the going was generally good enough to allow quite rapid manoeuvres with a 5-ton gun, but it was not the same in the mud of Russia or, in the later stages of the war, Belgium. Nevertheless, the 88mm was the deadliest weapon in the German armoury and it was mounted in tanks, as well as self-propelled guns of various kinds. These 88mm guns were not all the same by any means, some were high-velocity, some models had horizontal sliding breeches, others vertical blocks. Even the ammunition changed, only the calibre remaining constant. In order to keep them mobile the final versions were self-propelled and so moved out of the realm of anti-tank guns pure and simple and became armoured vehicles – outside the scope of this book.

Yet the 88mm was not allowed to carry the burden alone. With that astonishing capacity to diversify their design and manufacturing effort, even when the enemy was almost at the gates, the German Army Ordnance continued to introduce different anti-tank guns almost up to the end of the war. At a time when above all other considerations continuity of calibre and model was necessary, at a time when it was above all vital not to interrupt production, still the new designs were introduced. Progressive development of existing models would have paid off better – as the 88mm showed throughout its life – but the Germans were forever dabbling with the new, and often untried.

In 1943 another anti-tank gun design was introduced. This was a small, light, wheeled gun which quickly became nick-named the 'Püppchen' or 'Dolly'. It was meant as an improved and more

66

effective version of the Panzerschrek rocket-launcher. The Püppchen resembled a small gun with a light two-wheeled carriage, a shield, trail and muzzle-flash eliminator – all in miniature. Unloaded it weighed 230lb and had a thin-walled barrel just over 5ft long. It fired a special version of the Panzerschrek bomb which had a small cartridge case filled over the tail fins. The bomb was loaded into the breech in the same way as a normal shell and the breech closed by a simple swinging plate and latch. On firing, the rocket behaved in the same way as it did in the Panzerschrek but, because it was in a closed barrel, there was a build up of gas pressure behind it and so more muzzle-velocity; that meant that the gun was not truly recoilless, but the recoil was not enough to move 230lb by much. It was hoped that the velocity would go up enough to increase the effective range to 700m, but this was not realised and 300–400m would be more realistic, with most actions taking place at much less than that. The Püppchen was not made in large numbers. A few were used in France in 1944 where they were not particularly good and it is doubtful if they ever enjoyed the confidence of the German soldier.

A year later, in the autumn of 1944, yet another anti-tank gun appeared, again a smooth-bore but this time a much more refined and workmanlike design. It was called, rather clumsily, the 8cm PWK 8 H 63 and, had it been given a proper development cycle and reasonable priority of materials, it might well have become one of the best infantry anti-tank guns of the war. Unfortunately there was no time for this and with little testing and developing it went into production in December 1944 with a target of forty complete equipments in the first month and 220 a month thereafter, though neither figure was ever reached. The intention was to make it a new infantry gun and re-equip every battalion with it, but the factories were too battered by bombing and too short of power and materials to build more than a token number. The performance of the H 63 was quite good for the time. A maximum range of 700m was achieved and the battle range was 600m. The projectile was fin-stabilised and similar to the Panzerschrek bomb. The propellant system used the high-low pressure principle. There was a distinct step in the chamber, against which rested the front of the short cartridge case. The front of the case was closed with a perforated disc and this disc had a short spigot projecting from the centre of it. The spigot fitted into the tail of the bomb and held the case and bomb together. The breech was closed by a light vertical sliding block.

On firing, the gas pressure built up in the short cartridge case and passed through the perforations in the front disc to give a reasonably even and constant pressure in the barrel, much more so than in a conventional gun. This steady pressure was also lower than that of the conventional gun so that the barrel could be lighter and the bomb could be made of thin sheet steel with no fear of it collapsing or distorting while accelerating in the barrel. There was a large and efficient muzzle brake which reduced the recoil forces on the carriage and permitted a low all-up weight of 1,300lb in action.

The high-low pressure system is very efficient but has not yet produced a high-velocity gun, and the H 63 fired its bomb at 1,000ft/sec with a medium charge and 1,400 with a super charge. The gunner was protected by a small sloping shield which came well round to the sides and from the front looks strangely like some squared-off helmet of a jousting knight. The whole profile of the weapon was extremely low and close to the ground. Had it come earlier in the war, when sufficient time could have been given to developing it, the H 63 might well have been a great success and there is no doubt that in the fighting in Italy and northern France a light gun with the range and punch which it had would have been most effective and very troublesome to the Allied armour. As it happened, it was destined to have no influence on the war at all, indeed very few ever saw action and few survive today. It was an unwise decision to try and change to an entirely new and untried gun at that stage of the war. It is doubtful if it ever knocked out so much as one tank.

One weapon which did knock out a tank, and many more than one, was the Faustpatrone. This was the first real one-man, anti-tank weapon which was both portable and successful. It was first issued in late 1942 and its appearance in battle caused a minor revolution and brought the single soldier in the slit-trench up to somewhere near parity with the tank. Not only that, but it was also the forerunner of modern throw-away weapons and in simplicity, effectiveness and cost, it is still as good as many in service today. Only in regard to range was it defective.

The Faustpatrone or Panzerfaust was a small recoilless gun. The barrel was a simple steel tube 31·5in long and just under 2in in diameter. Inside it was a propelling charge of 3oz of gunpowder ignited by a simple flash cap let into a hole in the wall of the tube and struck by a spring-loaded rod held by a stud. The stud was the trigger, pushed free by the firer's thumb. The trigger mechanism was covered in transit by a thin steel cover which flipped up to become a backsight. A series of holes in it allowed for different elevations at different ranges. There was virtually nothing else to the launcher. The bomb had a lightly constructed warhead with a short tail. The warhead contained a 3½lb hollow charge, which penetrated between 7in and 8in of armour. The tail was a wooden boom with four flexible fins wrapped round the stem. The bomb was loaded by pushing it tail first into the tube, where it lodged against the propelling charge. Loaded, the total weight was 11½lb of which the bomb weighed fractionally under 7lb.

To fire, the trigger cover was first released by withdrawing a locking pin and then pulled up until it was at right angles to the tube. The one locking pin also held the bomb in place in the launch tube so that, at this stage of the firing operation, it behoved the firer not to shake or tip his launcher too violently, not that any danger would accrue thereby, he would merely drop his bomb and would have to pick it off the ground and reinsert it. It would not explode until fired. The launcher tube was then held under the right arm with the left hand immediately behind the 'muzzle' and the head craned down to take a sight. This was an uncomfortable posture while standing and not much easier while crouching or lying. In fact the lying position was the most difficult of all to achieve because the back of the tube had to point well clear of the firer's body in order for him to avoid the backblast. The 'foresight' was the curve of the largest diameter of the bomb, and the backsight one of the holes in the vertical cover. It was a short sight base, and not an easy one to use for a difficult shot, but it did well enough for the very short effective range.

The muzzle-velocity was 145ft per second, a little better than the fastest test cricket bowlers and the firer was cautioned to wear a steel helmet as the splinters from the warhead were dangerous. The fighting range was 30m, or 33yd, and short though it was, 33yd was far better than running up to the tank and throwing a Teller mine on to the rear deck. The early models of Panzerfaust were too crudely made and were unsafe to fire in some cases, but the design was progressively improved and the warhead improved. The range of the last versions was increased to 66yd, but beyond that the chance of a hit was always low. The trouble was that the tail of the bomb had such a short length of travel in the barrel that there was little hope of raising either velocity or accuracy. Nevertheless, it sufficed.

The warhead of the Panzerfaust was very powerful for its size. This was achieved by using cyclonite as the explosive. Normally cyclonite is only used in small quantities as an initiating charge since it is not too stable. The presence of several pounds of it in the Panzerfaust was a definite hazard and it had to be mixed with beeswax to prevent the molecules rubbing together on firing and producing enough energy to detonate the charge at the muzzle. Even so, there were accidents, and the majority of the Germans who fired the device were frankly terrified of it. The warhead could penetrate a remarkable thickness of armour. The jet was 5–6ft long and in one authenticated case in France in 1944 a

(*Opposite*) Four shoulder-fired anti-tank weapons:
A. The German Racketenpanzerbuchse of 1943. The large square shield is to protect the firer from back-blast. What appears to be a large hollow trigger is in fact the cocking handle for the electric firing mechanism;
B. An early production model of the US Bazooka. The round-nosed bomb is a late model, posed to show the difference between it and the pointed-nose first versions;
C. German Panzerfaust 60, the largest of the series to be taken into service in significant numbers. The sight has been raised and the trigger is cocked;
D. Soviet RPG-2 with its rocket. With this weapon the rocket is loaded from the muzzle and the warhead stays outside the tube.

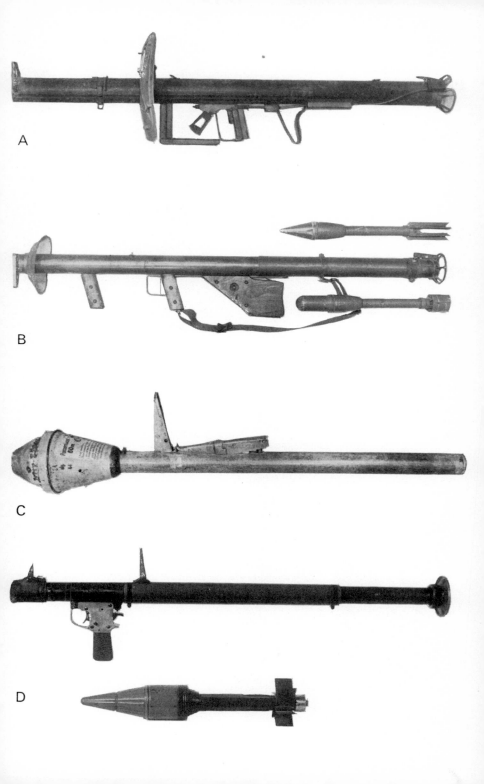

A

B

C

D

Page 72 (*right*)
Bob Burns the radio comedian and his original 'Bazooka' standing beside one of the early models of the rocket-launcher of the same name.

(*left*) An American soldier firing his M 72 rocket-launcher in Vietnam. The rocket has just left the muzzle and is out of the picture, but the blast has shaken the photographer so that the picture is blurred.

Sherman was hit in the side as it passed down a street in a small town. The jet passed right across the crew compartment killing the gunner, and passed out through the other side into the open air. There was considerable damage inside the tank, but only minor injuries, apart from the unfortunate gunner. In other instances Panzerfaust easily penetrated Sherman turrets, but there are no records of them going right through.

The Panzerfaust caused many tank casualties to the Allies and far more damaging was its morale effect. Tanks became wary of approaching close cover without a strong infantry escort, and even then a carefully concealed Panzerfaust gunner could bob up out of a ditch or from behind a tree. The results were sometimes out of proportion to the numbers of men involved. On 29 March 1945 a squadron of 1st RTR was held up for four hours by a small party of Germans who were concealed behind strong road blocks and armed with Panzerfausts. It wasn't that the squadron was lacking in nerve, but it simply was not worth trying to get too close until every Panzerfaust had been eliminated. Too many Shermans had been knocked out in the advance through France and the Low Countries for anyone to take foolhardy risks.

The Germans also tried aircraft anti-tank guns in much the same way as the British did with the Hurricane. There were several gun candidates for trial but the one which was the most successful was an automatic version of the 37mm PAK 35/36. This was produced by Rheinmetall in 1942, using the experience gained in the making of the 20mm Panzerbuchse 41 heavy anti-tank rifle. This 37mm gun was intended to be an AA weapon, and it had some success in that role although the range was too limited for it to be of any great value. It used the same principle of firing out of battery as did the Panzerbuchse 41, and so the recoil was reasonably low. Ammunition was the same as the PAK 35/36, with a special super-sensitive fuze for AA work and the rounds were fed into the breech in clips of six from the left-hand side. The action was unusually reliable – a fact which caused it to beat a competing design from Mauser – and this also led to the idea that the gun might be suitable for aircraft mounting. Low recoil and reliability were the two most needed virtues for a gun that was going to have to hang out on a wing in all weathers.

E

The Junkers 87 Stuka was chosen as a gun platform, partly because it was becoming distinctly dated in the dive-bomber role, and partly because it was strong, steady and could be flown at sufficiently slow speeds to give the pilot time to take a good aim. Two guns were mounted below the wing, one on each side outboard of the undercarriage legs. The breech was enclosed in a streamlined pod from which the feed housing stuck out. The gun was 10ft long overall and at least 6ft projected in front of the leading edge of the wing, giving an even stranger look to the ugly old Junkers. Despite the few rounds of ammunition in each magazine, the guns were highly effective. The favoured method of attack was to locate the target by flying over the battlefield at a fairly low height, say 4,000–5,000ft, roll over and dive on to the selected tank from a steep angle. Tracer-firing machine-guns were used to correct the point of aim and the instant it was on the target, the pilot let go with his 37mm guns. Normally one round from each was all that was required to knock out a tank, though two or more could be fired if necessary. Even the T-34 was vulnerable to this form of attack and rarely needed more than two rounds to finish it off. The great exponent of the Stuka attack was a Major Rudel, still alive today, who flew the incredible total of 2,530 sorties on the Eastern Front between 1942 and 1945 and who is officially credited with a score of 519 tanks and over a thousand lesser armoured vehicles. Rudel was obviously a man with stamina beyond the normal for he frequently flew five or six sorties a day for days on end without proper rest and survived endless attacks from Russian fighters and AA guns. He is one of the highest decorated pilots of the Luftwaffe – and with good reason.

These anti-tank JU 87s started in a unit called the Experimental Anti-Tank Air Detachment which soon became the 9th Ground Attack Wing of the 4th Air Group, and a varying number of squadrons was attached at one time or another, but the usual average was six. Of these, two were Focke-Wolfe 190s fitted with two 30mm cannon, and the other four were a mixture of JU 87s, JU 88s and Henschel 129s. The JU 88 was not a success in the anti-tank role and was soon abandoned. It carried a single 50mm variant of the PAK 38 or a 75mm. Neither worked well in an aeroplane and the machine itself was not suited to the method of attack needed for tanks. The Henschel 129 was another story, however. This machine, which saw little service on the Western Front, was a low-wing, twin-engined, ground-attack fighter. Although not particularly fast nor manoeuvrable it could survive against the slow Soviet fighters and so was fitted with two 30mm Mauser MK 101 cannon. The MK 101 had first been intended as an air-to-air weapon, but it was found to have far more potential in the anti-tank role. The tungsten-carbide, anti-armour round would penetrate the back and top armour of the Soviet tanks with ease and, as in the JU 87, a machine-gun was used to ensure a hit with the first burst. On 8 July 1943 the 4th Air Group completely repelled a surprise Soviet counter-attack by an armoured brigade which came in behind the 1st SS Panzer Corps. For one hour, four Henschel squadrons of the Group maintained squadron-sized attacks on the Soviet armour and forced them to withdraw without any German ground troops taking any part in the action at all. The majority of the attacking force was destroyed and left burning on the battlefield. In another battle, that of the Orel River Bend in 1943, the 4th Group flew 37,421 sorties in which it claimed to have knocked out 1,100 tanks and 1,300 wheeled and tracked vehicles. These are astonishing figures but the claims of pilots were checked as carefully as possible and they are undoubtedly close to the truth; what they do show, however, is the grave vulnerability of the tank to a properly armed ground-attack aeroplane enjoying freedom of the skies to choose its time and method of attack.

The final weapon to see service in the Wehrmacht, and almost the last one to appear was, incredible though it seems, another anti-tank rifle. This was the Mss 41, a Czech design from the ZB factory in Brno. Not very much is known about its history although a few specimens have survived the war. The figure '41' would seem to indicate 1941 as its starting date, but it was not seen in action until 1944. The likelihood is that the ZB works made a small stock in the heyday of anti-tank rifles and left them in store. Why they were brought out so late in the war is a complete mystery.

As a defence against tanks the Mss 41 was naturally useless, but as an example of weapon design it is fascinating. The gun is a 'bull-pup' layout, with the magazine behind the pistol grip and trigger. The magazine feeds upwards and there is no bolt as with conventional weapons. There is a buffer against the shoulder pad and a 'bolt head' complete with locking lugs on the front of it. A hammer and firing pin is tucked behind it. Riding over the rear end of the barrel is a loose locking sleeve which engages with the lugs on the front of the buffer, and also engages with other lugs on the barrel. This sleeve acts as a sort of enlarged locking nut which holds the barrel against the breech face. To reload, the pistol grip is rotated to the right, an action which unlocks the lugs. The pistol grip is then smartly pushed forward and the barrel moves forward with it, uncovering the empty case which remains held firmly to the bolt head by the extractor claws. At the forward point of movement, or just before it, the empty case is ejected and a fresh round is pushed up from the magazine.

The pistol grip is now pulled back, dragging the barrel and breech over the next round and a twist to the left brings the grip back to the vertical and locks the action. Whilst there are all manner of advantages to this system, there are about as many equal disadvantages, not the least of which is a susceptibility to the effects of dust and dirt. There is also too much freedom in the barrel bearings, allowing wear, which would straightaway affect accuracy. However, one must take off one's hat to ZB for originality: it was one of the shortest and lightest anti-tank rifles ever made. In 1938 it would have been a phenomenon; in 1944 it was a flop.

This then is the story of those German anti-tank weapons of World War II which actually saw service. If one had to sum up the whole saga in a few words, it would perhaps be fair to say that it is a history of immense imagination, ingenuity, innovation and boldness – both in design and in battlefield use – but hampered by production difficulties not always the result of a weapon's designers and by a superfluity of ideas and models, few of which were developed logically.

There was also an entire shadow world of esoteric ideas which never saw the light of day, or which never survived more than the scantiest testing. Some of these we examine in another chapter.

4

THE ENGLISH-SPEAKING UNION, BRITAIN AND AMERICA

A tank is the best means of defence against another tank . . .
Anon

Italy entered the war in June 1940 confident that she had done so in time to pick up some of the pieces left from the fighting, yet not too soon as to be closely engaged. She miscalculated; the end was four years away and the journey to it would be expensive and embarrassing. Within a couple of months General Wavell had started the Desert War by attacking the Italian outposts on the Egyptian frontier and soon after the first of the advances along the North African coastline began. In the coming years the British public was to become accustomed to the steady ebb and flow of fortune along that coastal strip as first one side and then the other gained the upper hand; the action swung back and forth. In this initial clash the contestants were lightly equipped, later on the desert became the trial ground for many new equipments.

For this first action the British were carrying the familiar 2-pounder and the Boys rifle. The 2-pounders were for the most part in the tanks, though the infantry did have their quota. The Italians had the M.11 tank and a few Model 35 47mm anti-tank guns. For the most part, however, they had to rely on artillery for anti-tank defence, and several guns were sited well forward for this purpose – not unlike the arrangements made by the German Army in 1917–18. They were not enough. Early in the morning of 9 December 1940 7th RTR attacked Sidi Barrani in conjunction with the 4th Indian Division. Within ten minutes 23 Italian M.11 tanks were knocked out and many set on fire by the fire of the 2-pounders of 7 RTRs Matildas. Meanwhile, the Italian artillery shells bounced off the slow-moving Matildas and reduced the defenders to despair. Even the 47mm guns were useless – mainly because of bad handling it must be admitted, rather than from any actual deficiency in the gun. Two months later, after the battle of Beda Fomm which took place between 5 and 7 February 1941, it was found that 101 Italian tanks had been left on the battlefield. Of these forty-eight had been hit and put out of action by 2-pounder shells, but it must be remembered that they were M.13s with very thin and inadequate armour.

When the first German tanks arrived the 2-pounder still had the edge on them to some extent. The Panzer Mk III mounted a 50mm short gun, the Kwk, and the 2-pounder had better penetration for less muzzle blast and flash. The trouble was that at ranges above 1,000yd the 2-pounder was useless whereas the Kwk could still throw an effective HE shell; hence, if the 2-pounder was located, the Mk IIIs simply stood off and shelled it with HE until it was destroyed. Nevertheless, the 2-pounder could defeat the turret, lower hull and the sides of all the medium German tanks that were in the Western Desert in 1941, and furthermore could do it at 1,000yd. The 50mm shells of the Mk III bounced off the Matildas and Crusaders of the RTR. But the day of the 2-pounder was waning swiftly. However, there was nothing for it but to go on using it until a better gun was issued and the pleas of the desert infantrymen put renewed life into the slow-moving plans for the production of the 6-pounder, which had laid pretty well dormant since 1938. Although 400 of these guns were ordered in June of 1940, they could not be built until 1941 and the first issues did not reach the desert until mid-1942.

In the meantime the 2-pounder was given a new lease of life by putting it on a lorry – the 'Portee mounting'. This mounting used a 15cwt truck with the sides taken off the back so that it had a flat bed. Using two long ramps a 2-pounder was hauled up and set down on its platform. The wheels were removed and bolted on the sides of the truck. The gun could be fired from the flat bed or it could be unloaded and emplaced. By reversing the truck up to the emplacement and throwing down the ramps, it could be evacuated quite quickly, although it could not be done with safety by daylight. The idea gave the little 2-pounders some much-needed mobility and the Portee gunners soon evolved a technique in which they lay up behind a low mound with only the top of the shield and the barrel emerging round the side of the cover. This was safe enough until the tank moved to a flank whereupon the unfortunate truck began to catch the shot and the gun had to move. One anti-tank regiment lost almost a complete battery in one day early in 1942. When the first of the 6-pounders arrived, they too were mounted as Portees, though they were getting a little heavy for continuously pulling up and down the ramps.

The 6-pounder was one of the memorable guns of World War II. It was small enough to be manhandled yet large enough to be effective until the monster tanks came at the end of the war. It was a gun with which the gunner felt himself to be a part of the mechanism, rather as a rifleman does when firing his rifle. The 6-pounder had a free traverse, controlled by the gunner's shoulder and this made the task of tracking moving targets far easier than if it had to be done by turning a hand wheel. He merely leaned in the direction he wanted the barrel to move. On firing, the recoil was reasonably light and so easy to handle that firing it was a positive pleasure. Another great virtue in the eyes of the crew was that it was very low and only needed a shallow pit to conceal it. Digging in anti-tank guns has never been a recreation of the British soldier.

At first the infantry were sceptical of its possibilities, but its first action dispelled any doubts. The 4th Indian Division was dug in along the Alamein position and on the night of 16 July 1942 5 Infantry Brigade was attacked by an armoured force for three hours. In the light of day next morning the brigade looked out at a battlefield strewn with the wreckage of 24 tanks, 6 armoured cars, 1 self-propelled assault gun, 5 20mm AA guns,

5 37mm anti-tank guns, 8 75mm field guns and 6 88mm AA guns which had been used as anti-tank guns. For all this impressive total of damage the 6-pounders of 5 Brigade had been largely responsible and in the words of the official history: 'In a day these venomous little cannon became the pride of the Eighth Army.'

Three months later there was another contest which settled the fame of the 6-pounder for the rest of the war. This was the 'Snipe' or Kidney Ridge battle which took place on 27 October in the southern half of the Alamein position, just before the break-out of the Eighth Army. The troops who fought this heroic action were the 2nd Battalion the Rifle Brigade, most of 239 Battery, Royal Artillery, and some men of the Royal Engineers. The battalion had its own anti-tank platoon armed with 6-pounders and the battery was similarly armed. There were no other effective anti-tank weapons in the force. There were plenty of machine-guns because this was a motor battalion and although it had fewer men than the usual infantry battalion it had more vehicles and far higher fire-power. As it fell out it was just as well that things were that way.

The plan was for the force to make a night dash into enemy-held territory and seize and hold a certain position until daylight when they would be relieved by a brigade-sized force who would then mount a series of offensive operations from this 'firm base'. The position was given the code name of 'Snipe' and there was some uncertainty about its exact location, though it was known from the existing maps to be well over a mile from the front line and in an area well populated with an active enemy protected by mine fields. The night was moonless and, after being deflected from the most direct route by the mine fields, the battalion finally dug in on a flat plain some little way from the real 'Snipe'. They were in the middle of several tank laager and it was not long before the aggressive Riflemen began to stir them up. By dawn, when the first attacks began, there were about 300 men in the position with nineteen 6-pounders and plenty of machine-guns and machine-gun ammunition. Unfortunately – and this was not to be a serious matter until later in the day when the force had been marooned for some hours – there was too little ammunition for the 6-pounders, but this was not realised in the excitement of the black night with the growling and clanking of disturbed German armour on all sides.

Throughout the following day the little force was continuously attacked by Italian and German armour and infantry. Incredibly they held out. The relief force was unable to cross the open desert to help, though some vehicles did manage to slip through in the other direction carrying wounded back from 'Snipe'; but any move forward by the brigade was immediately broken up by concentrated and furious fire from hull-down tanks and self-propelled guns. Steadily the ammunition stocks sank, steadily the numbers of blackened wrecks grew around 'Snipe', and steadily the numbers of effective fighting men grew less within the position. By a combination of courage and skilful technique the anti-tank gunners continued to knock out enemy tanks all day, but attrition took its toll and for each attack there were fewer guns than for the last. For the most part the gunners held their fire until the last possible moment, often when the tanks were less than 50yd away. At that range even a Mark IV could be knocked out first shot, and most of them caught fire immediately. Frequently the tanks had no idea where the guns were until they opened fire and by then it was too late. The gun crews could get off three or four shots at as many tanks before any one of them could locate the 6-pounder, traverse his turret, lay an aim, and fire.

The handiness of the gun was never more clearly shown. The loader could throw shells into the breech almost as fast as he could pick them up; the layer could traverse rapidly by using his shoulder to swing the barrel round and with tanks at such short range there was no need to alter the elevation at all – the layer merely switched his aim from tank to tank while his loader slammed in another round every time the gun fired. In those conditions a shot every three or four seconds is perfectly possible – but only for three or four. It cannot be kept up for long. Not every tank was hit at close range, however. At some stages of the battle it became necessary to engage tanks forming up to attack the relief force which were 1,200yd or more away. Most of those fired at were hit and knocked out, either temporarily or permanently. Few escaped the 6-pounders, but by the end of the afternoon the ammunition was almost exhausted and at this

81

stage it is appropriate to quote the words of C. E. Lucas-Phillips's book *Alamein*.

> The enemy, however, Germans and Italians alike, had now had quite enough. The scene of desolation in and around the outpost was staggering. Nearly seventy tanks and self-propelled guns, all but seven of them being of the enemy, lay wrecked or derelict, many still burning and the black smoke from their fuel trailing forlornly across the desert. To these were added the shattered remains of several tracked and wheeled vehicles. Hanging out of the open turrets of the tanks, or concealed within their bowels, were the charred corpses of their crews who had been unable to escape the flames. Around them sprawled the bodies of those caught by the Riflemen's machine guns. Within or immediately on the perimeter of the island were seven British tanks and one German, and the wreckage of sixteen Bren-carriers, several jeeps and ten guns. Five other guns had been damaged; out of the original nineteen, not more than six remained that could be relied upon to engage.
>
> Within this panorama of desolation and death there still remained however, some 200 gallant men, red-eyed, coated with dirt and sweat, hungry and thirsty, but their spirit even higher than when they had first set out. Within their desert keep, as the crimson sun began to damp down its fires and to tinge with blood the funereal plumes of smoke from the dead tanks, they waited calmly with their few remaining guns and their last rounds of ammunition for a final attack which never came.

That night the Riflemen withdrew, carrying their wounded and the breech-blocks of their guns. They had shown the tanks were helpless against good anti-tank guns properly and bravely manned (as indeed they still are), and they had shown that the new 6-pounder was more than a match for any German tank and that by using it properly infantry could defend themselves against any armoured assault.

The 'Snipe' action gained such fame that it was examined by a special committee who conducted their enquiry on the actual site and supported all but the most extravagant claims. Seventy-two Riflemen and gunners of all ranks were killed or wounded and an unknown number of Royal Engineers. The losses to the enemy must have been far greater, since few tank crews survived and many infantry were killed by machine-gun fire. One VC and one DSO were awarded, together with three DCMs and several MCs and MMs.

Its size also made the 6-pounder ideal for airborne use. By sheer good luck the Horsa glider was made with a fuselage wide enough to take the 6-pounder with a modified carriage and the jeep which towed it – so the anti-tank defence of the airborne divisions was assured. After several unsuccessful trials the 6-pounder was also parachuted from the Halifax bomber which carried it as an external load under the bomb-bay. For parachuting, some minor modifications were made and the gun was supported in a strong crate on to which the parachute slings and crash pans were attached. In order to prevent the unwieldy load from somersaulting as it fell away, it had to be dropped in a nose-down attitude from the plane and this ensured a clean break-away. Failure to do this and the gun flipped over backwards cutting its attachment cables, or at best wrapping them around itself, and the entire equipment 'candled' in to the drop zone digging itself into the ground with an appalling crash. Even the 6-pounder, robust though it was, could not survive that sort of treatment.

While the 6-pounder maintained the general anti-tank defence of the infantry, there was still no adequate close-range weapon for the individual soldier or the small infantry sections and platoons. The Boys rifle remained in issue – and indeed in manu-facture – until 1943, by which time BSA had made 69,000 of them but they were unpopular because of their weight and relative ineffectiveness. In the early days of the desert campaign, the Boys did have a few successes against the flimsy Italian light tanks but few infantrymen had any faith in it. When the infant airborne units asked for some protection from armoured vehicles, they were offered the Boys, with a cut-down barrel so that it fitted into a weapons' container. Six inches had to be removed, and with it went the muzzle brake. As a result, it was most unpleasant to fire and unpopular with the troops. The parachutists used it for a short time, then dropped it in favour of the PIAT, of which more shortly. Some armoured cars fitted a Boys rifle on to their turrets to give a better punch than their Vickers machine-guns, and a few rifles were even mounted on top of the Universal (Bren) carrier. In Malaya a badly harassed battalion of the Indian Army, the 1/14th Punjabis, retreating before the Japanese advance, used its Boys rifles on a pair of

83

light tanks trying to rush a road block. Both the tanks were knocked out and their crews captured, but this sort of action was rare. For the most part the anti-tank rifles of 1940 and 1941 were totally inadequate for their intended task.

The British response to this inadequacy was to find some way of firing a larger version of the 68 grenade. The 68 had been a good grenade, although very little used in action, but the grenade principle of using a discharger cup on a rifle made for too light a projectile and too short a range. Several designers bent their minds to the task and the most promising system looked to be one using the same spigot principle as on the Blacker Bombard. Two prototypes appeared in 1941, both very similar in appearance and principle. One was designed by a man named Watts, the other by Jeffries. The launchers were tubes of thin sheet steel containing the firing spring and trigger mechanism. At the front was a trough to hold the bomb and the spigot projected down the middle of the trough. At the other end of the tube was a shoulder pad. Simple aperture sights were fitted. The bombs had a hollow tail boom with a small cartridge at the front end. The warhead was a hollow charge, the Jeffries being larger than the Watts.

On firing, the spigot passed up the tail boom and fired the cartridge. This launched the bomb which flew off the spigot and on its way to the target. Meanwhile, the force of the explosion moved the spigot back against its spring and recocked it. The moment the first bomb had left, another could be slipped into the trough and the shooting continued. There were several advantages to this system. First of all, it did not rely on a precision barrel or any high-grade materials, which made it popular with the Ministry of Production. Secondly, there was little muzzle blast, which made it easier to conceal. Thirdly, it could accommodate a fair-sized warhead as there were no real calibre restrictions to worry about. The system was adopted and the production version was a meld of the Watts and Jeffries designs. It was given the clumsy and rather pompous title of Projector, Infantry, Anti-Tank, which was only used in official documents. To everyone who ever dealt with it, it was the PIAT.

One feature of spigot mortars is that they have to have their spigot cocked before they can fire. With the PIAT this had to be done by hand and a fearful job it was. There were two methods. The gunner could stand up, hold the PIAT upright beside him, bend over and grasp the trigger guard with both hands. Then with both feet on the shoulder pad, he straightened his body and pulled the spigot down into the gun until he heard the trigger sear click on to it. He was pulling against a 200lb spring to do this. He could then relax and push the casing back down over the now compressed spring. This method took the muscles of a Hercules and was a fruitful source of strained backs. The second method was hardly less exhausting, but not so damaging to the back; it was meant to be used when in a trench. The gunner lay down on his side, held the trigger guard close up to his chest, and pushed away with both legs looking somewhat like a recumbent athlete wrestling with a grotesque pogo stick. Neither method was easy, nor very practicable in the face of the enemy.

The PIAT could also be used as a crude mortar. The shoulder pad could be rotated through 90° and laid on the ground to give more elevation, and the monopod leg lengthened for the same reason. At full stretch just over 300yd could be obtained, with rather doubtful accuracy but a satisfying crump at the other end. The intention was to knock out bunkers and machine-gun posts.

The PIAT had to be held very firmly for firing. The right hand controlled the trigger – and all fingers were needed to move it – while the left hand reached forward to the front of the trigger guard and pulled back on it for all it was worth. When the trigger was released, there was a short pause while the spigot ran forward, and in this interval it was vital that the firer kept his firm hold. Unwary recruits who did not were dealt a staggering blow on the shoulder by the recoil and left with an uncocked spigot to contemplate. The firer who hung on was firstly partially deafened by the cartridge (as indeed was his loader), then pushed hard backwards while the spring clanked down the casing and recocked. It was an easy weapon to fire and maintain, but not one to treat carelessly.

It has spawned a whole series of legends, not all of them apocryphal. One which I particularly like concerns a certain battalion of the Guards Armoured Division in northern France in the summer of 1944. This battalion, like many others at that time, had snipers on its establishment, men of individual character who were given plenty of freedom in how they fought their war and who often did it in unconventional ways. One day two snipers – let us call them Black and White for the sake of anonymity since one at least is now a director of a respected City company – decided that as the sniping trade was suffering a temporary slump they would fill in a few hours by sniping at a tank. With no more thought about it than that they borrowed a PIAT, persuaded the owner to cock it for them, picked up a carrier of three bombs and set off for the sharp end. Black was in the lead with the PIAT with White humping the bombs behind.

They were lucky in that there was a Tiger making life unpleasant for one of the leading companies and even luckier in that it was sitting on the edge of a cornfield so that it could be stalked through the cover of the corn. Now there was one feature of the Tiger which is germane to this story: the turret had to be traversed by hand and several tons of turret and gun took a lot of rotating with only a hand wheel. Not only that, but it also took a bit of stopping once it had got up speed. It used to be said that, given a stationary Tiger on level ground manned by a determined crew, an unarmed man of reasonable fitness could defeat it simply by running steadily round and round the tank at a range of 50yd or so, keeping ahead of the gun until the crew dropped from exhaustion. A bit far-fetched, but a happy thought.

After an hour of effort our intrepid pair had crawled almost to within 100yd of the Tiger, when Black popped his head up for a look and realised that they had been spotted. The huge turret was turning towards them and the long gun barrel was foreshortening with frightening speed as it slewed round. There was nothing for it but to risk a hurried shot. 'Quick,' he hissed over his shoulder to White, 'give me a bomb.' Instantly there was an urgent noise of rustling and muttering in the corn stalks and the sound of lids popping off cardboard bomb containers. 'Christ,' wailed White, 'run for it, I've brought an empty bloody carrier!'

They still tell the story at regimental reunions.

But the PIAT had one great advantage that has not yet been regained in modern weapons. It had little muzzle flash and no back-blast and so was perfectly safe to fire in confined spaces such as houses. In the desperate street fighting in Arnhem when one battalion of the Parachute Regiment held the vital road bridge against repeated armoured attacks, it was the PIAT which took the brunt of the fighting. Although originally intended to be an interim weapon, the PIAT stayed in service almost until the Korean War. It was never particularly popular, mainly because its range was only 100yd and it weighed 32lb. Not only that, but it was unwieldy, awkward and difficult to carry.

While the PIAT was undergoing its early trials and misfortunes, another method of attacking tanks was being tried in the Western Desert. From the very first days of the fighting, aircraft had been used against vehicles in one way or another. As early as 14 December 1940 several armoured cars of the 11th Hussars were knocked out by Italian fighters as they prepared to descend the escarpment near the Bardia–Tobruk road. There was no effective defence in the armoured column against air attack, and presumably the fighters were using bombs and 20mm cannon. With the excellent visibility which could be obtained in the desert, it seemed sensible to try to exploit the swift mobility of the aeroplane in seeking out tanks. Accordingly the idea of the 'tank-busting' aeroplane was born. Luckily there was a gun on hand which was eminently suitable for the job. This was the Vickers 40mm Class 'S'; the gun design had been started in 1938 and it was originally intended for air-to-air fighting. By early 1940, however, when successful trials had been carried out, experience had shown that 40mm shells were unlikely to destroy an aircraft with one hit, and further work on the gun was relegated to a low priority. Early in 1941 it was decided to install the Vickers 40mm gun in a Beaufighter for air trials. In the meantime the Hawker Aircraft Co commenced the design of a special Hurricane (Mark IID) to take two 40mm guns – one under each wing. The first Hurricane so equipped was sent for trials in September 1941. The trials, which included a demonstration against a Valentine tank, confirmed the suitability of the installation for the attack of Armoured Fighting

87

Vehicles (AFVs). It was decided to equip one squadron in the Middle East with the anti-tank Hurricanes, and No 6 Squadron was chosen. Re-equipment took place in April 1942 and from then until the end of the year the squadron took part in many operations against enemy tank formations with conspicuous success.

The gun originally had a fifteen-round magazine, but this was considered inadequate, so Vickers designed a magazine to hold thirty rounds, and also a belt-feed mechanism. The former was found to be too bulky for wing installation and the project was dropped, but the latter became a standard fitment. There were other changes too. The floor of the cockpit and the underside of the engine were armoured sufficiently to keep out small-arms fire at close range. The standard reflector sight was harmonised for the 40mm guns at a range of 800yd, and other armament was removed.

The 40mm guns were both fired together, producing a drop in flying speed of at least 40mph. Should one gun jam, the other had to be cut immediately; otherwise, the off-centre recoil could flip the Hurricane on to its back. The attacking height was about 10ft above ground level, which left no room for errors in flying! But the results were worth it for the 40mm solid-shot projectiles did good work against the side armour of Axis tanks and the usual method of attack was to try to find a laager and catch the tanks in mass with their engines stopped. The Hurricanes could then sweep in from 2,000yd out into the desert, lining up exactly on a selected tank and open fire at 700yd or less. However, they were good targets for ground gunners, particularly those firing 20mm Flak equipments and the losses from flak were high. So too were crack-ups from flying accidents and though the squadron ran up an impressive score of tanks knocked out or damaged, when the fighting moved on to Tunisia, they were rearmed and relegated to shipping protection. The idea was not tried again in that form.

It was renewed in a slightly different form later in the war. In 1944 another RAF fighter, the Typhoon, was fitted with anti-vehicle rockets for ground-attack work. The Typhoon was larger and heavier than the Hurricane and it operated in northern

Page 89　(above) A captured Japanese 37mm anti-tank gun on Makin Island in 1943. There is a machine-gun tripod, which would not normally be there, tied to the trail; (below) The Belgian Blindicide rocket-launcher. The length of the tube is most noticeable and the conical face shield is typical of the Blindicide family.

Page 90 (*above*) The Canadian Heller rocket-launcher. The range-finder sight, which distinguishes this weapon from all others in its class, is on top of the barrel; (*below*) A British soldier demonstrating the firing position of the Energa grenade when fired from the British L1A1 rifle.

France, not over the desert. The usual method of attack was in a shallow dive rather than a flat approach and the dangers were lessened and the casualties fewer. The rockets were both large and heavy, being based on a 3in diameter rocket-motor tube. This tube was 6ft long and the warhead was screwed on to the end of it. The first warheads were 5in naval shells of an obsolete pattern, but these were quickly replaced by a special design of simpler construction with a thinner wall. The weight of these heads was 20lb and later models went up to 60lb.

The rockets were carried on rails slung under the wings and fired electrically either singly, in ripples, or in one salvo. Typhoons could carry a full load of twelve, and this gave them formidable fire-power. A hit on a tank was enough to almost completely destroy it and at Falaise in Normandy in July 1944 the rocket-firing Typhoons caused a monumental holocaust among retreating German motorised columns. But the RAF was never entirely happy about the rockets, even though they remained in service for many years after the war. In fact, they were relatively inaccurate and the enormous damage at Falaise tended to conceal the fact that single targets were extremely difficult to hit. The roads in Normandy had been crammed with vehicles and it was almost impossible to miss provided that the plane was pointed roughly in the right direction; a solitary tank was another proposition and often an inordinate number of rockets were needed before it was hit. There was therefore a continuous demand for faster and more accurate projectiles, though the war ended before they arrived.

Meanwhile the rockets attracted considerable attention. On one airfield in France the Typhoons changed over from 20lb warheads to 60lb, and this meant a complete change of mounting. A small pile of discarded launch rails grew up beside the airfield as the change went on. A platoon of the Guards Armoured Division enquired the reason and on learning why, promptly commandeered the scrapped rails and some 20-pounder rockets. The rails were welded to the sides of the turret of a few tanks by the unit fitters, and an improvised firing circuit set up. Some days later the advance was held up by a single Royal Tiger enfiladed behind a barn. One of the rocket-firing tanks was brought up and fired a ripple of four which disintegrated the Tiger with one blast. Within hours every RAF airfield in the area was besieged by scrounging guardsmen demanding rockets. But they were misled because the one demonstration, effective though it was, could never be repeated. The rockets flew too slowly to have more than a slight chance of hitting anything when fired from a stationary launcher. In the air they had the additional speed of the plane which carried them, and even so the RAF found them barely satisfactory. But they were to be seen on the turrets of many tanks until the close country of the Reichswehr Forest forced their crews to take them off.

Throughout the Western Desert campaign, the British were outranged by the German tank guns. This led to several embarrassing and dangerous incidents when tanks were able to knock out the anti-tank defence without harm to themselves and advance right into the British defended localities. Since this meant that they also came uncomfortably close to the artillery gun lines, the gunners took care to defend themselves and an anti-tank projectile was produced for the 25-pounder field gun. This was a solid shot of no great sophistication but possessing considerable momentum. Its calibre was 3·45in, or 88mm, a point which Allied propagandists missed completely. To give it the greatest possible muzzle-velocity it was only fired with Charge Super, and this placed an unacceptable strain on the buffer-recuperator system. A muzzle brake was therefore quickly introduced, and all guns were threaded at the muzzle to accept it. The solid shot was most effective and, the moment this was realised by the infantry, the gunners found themselves being persuaded to come forward with a fervour never before known in their history. Quite naturally this did not go well with the plans of artillery commanders farther back, who had few enough guns as it was for their tasks, without losing them in the anti-tank battle. It was foolish of the infantry to ask for them anyway, because the guns which are going to throw shrapnel and high explosive in front of your position when the attack comes in, need to be in a different place from the guns which make holes in the tanks. But there were times in the desert when the normal priorities of war became a little blurred by the harassments of the moment.

The desert had shown that the German tank was gaining the upper hand over the British anti-tank gun, and the 6-pounder, despite its pleasant characteristics, was being rapidly outmatched. The infantry soon demanded a bigger gun and the designers duly got to work. The answer was to select a shell weighing nearly three times as much, namely 17lb. The initial work had begun in early 1941 when it was foreseen that sooner or later a heavier gun would be needed, so that when the requirement came, the main part of the design work was already done. The 17-pounder was produced in an incredibly short space of time. Legend has it that it was one year from the first demand to the first batch going into action, but this seems apocryphal and it was more likely to have been three months longer than that. However, the gun was first used in its infantry version at the battle of the Mareth Line in March 1943 when the first production batch, hurried out to be in time for the battle, gave the German Tiger tanks a severe beating.

The gun weighed nearly $2\frac{1}{2}$ tons and in the design stages this weight had disturbed the infantry who felt that it would be difficult to manhandle. Although not easy to move, it was found that the crew could manage to drag it for short distances and it was not impossible to dig it in and conceal it. The chief trouble that the infantry encountered was in finding a vehicle to tow it. Jeeps could tow a 6-pounder but it was asking for trouble to hitch 4,600lb behind a vehicle that had been designed to pull 1,000lb. In the end it came down to either a 3-ton truck or a large tracked carrier and these were few and far between. In the battle of the Wadi Akrit in April 1943, 50 RTR used their tanks to tow sixteen guns on to the objective so that the infantry had adequate anti-tank defence against the German counter-attacks. It was not the last time that tanks would be used to get the guns up, and the transport problem was not adequately solved until after the war.

The 17-pounder was in effect a scaled-up 6-pounder, though many differences had to be introduced to cope with the greater strength and weight. The free traverse of the 6-pounder was abandoned, the ammunition could no longer be so easily tossed about, and concealment was far more of a problem particularly after the first shot – the muzzle blast was enormous and the noise terrifying. There was a certain amount of grumbling at first, but the crews soon came to realise that this was an effective gun which could take on a Tiger at almost any range and see it off and it continued to do so until the last days of the war when the monster tanks appeared in France and Holland.

At 1,000yd the 17-pounder could penetrate the front and turret of all medium tanks, and the side armour of the heavy tanks. At 500yd the front armour of the Tiger was in danger. Even at 2,000yd the shell could still do a great deal of damage to tracks and outside stowage, though no crew would think of starting the action so far out. As a self-propelled gun the 17-pounder was an immediate success. Fitted into the turret of the Sherman it proved to be a formidable combination and gave that under-gunned tank a punch that it should have had in the first place. By 1944 it had become so popular that there were not enough to fill all the demands and the ordnance factories were working at full capacity.

In addition to the Sherman mounting, the 17-pounder was also put into the Valentine as an SP gun, and later the Comet – though only in very small numbers on this chassis. In various guises the gun saw the war out and remained in service with the infantry until replaced by the BAT series in the middle 1950s. The School of Infantry ran the last 17-pounder course in 1956. Thirteen years is no bad record for a wartime gun; no other came near it.

On the other battle front in Tunisia the First Army was rather less well equipped for anti-tank warfare, and suffered accordingly. The exception was the Bazooka whose story is told in the American section of this book, but for the British the situation was far from good. The Parachute Brigade had hand-grenades and the Boys rifle. The grenade was the Gammon, invented by a captain of that name for anti-tank use. It was a stockinet bag with a contact fuze in one end. The fuze was the same as that in the No 69 grenade. It contained a steel marble which was freed on throwing and when the grenade struck a solid object, the steel ball jarred against a detonator and set off the charge. The bottom of the bag was open and could be filled with explosive. Every para-chutist carried 2lb of plastic explosive for this purpose and the great attraction of the idea was that the size of the charge could be suited to the purpose in hand. They were used on several occasions and the following account from *The Red Beret* by Hilary St George Saunders is typical:

> The enemy column hove into sight and the parachutists awaited it, every man having been ordered to hold his fire until the leading vehicle struck a mine. It was one of the armoured cars, and it duly did so; it then rammed the side of the hill, thus blocking the road. The two scout cars behind it received a volley of Gammon bombs and burst into flames; their occupants, four in each, were killed and cremated.

Grenades are dangerous weapons and some of the throwers in that small action were wounded by their own missiles.

This may be an appropriate moment to divert and mention the vulnerability of armoured vehicles to anti-tank measures. The subject is not a pleasant one, but it is germane to the study and an understanding of it will enable the reader who is unfamiliar with the subject to see why different vehicles respond in different ways to being attacked. Armoured cars were all thinly armoured and driven by petrol engines; they were therefore easily set on fire and really presented no great difficulty to any anti-tank gun. Tanks were another matter. The German tanks were all petrol-engined, except for some of the esoteric models at the end of the war, but were generally well armoured so that the gunner had to choose his point of aim with a little care. Once hit in a vital place, the German tank usually brewed up fairly quickly and the Panther had the unpleasant habit of actually blowing up when properly hit. British tanks varied. Valentines were tough nuts to crack and usually gave their crews time to get out. Shermans carried the reputation of being fire-bombs and it was said that the crew had five seconds to jump out of a penetrated Sherman before the flames were sucked into the crew compartment and they were caught. Churchills burnt slowly, giving their crews plenty of time to escape. The Russians were not only well armoured, but diesel-driven as well. They were extremely difficult to knock out.

In 1945 the British Army relied for its anti-tank defence upon three major weapons. These were the PIAT, the 6-pounder – still in service in many units – and the 17-pounder which was on a variety of mountings, both towed and SP. It seems an inadequate list and indeed it was, but the main anti-tank defence of the Army had for some time been the British tanks themselves. It became a popular saying that 'the best anti-tank defence is another tank', which is not true, but in the last months of the war it was a convenient and appropriate argument since there were plenty of Shermans and plenty of ammunition for them. So the infantry relied upon there always being enough tanks to pull them out of any tight spot and by a mixture of good luck and the mass production of the United States, the formula rarely failed. One place where it did fall down was the airborne assault on Arnhem, where the only tanks were German. Immediately the inadequacies of the 6-pounder were shown up in no uncertain way and the Panzers were only kept at bay by feats of heroism by the crews of the few guns that survived and the men who carried the PIATs. It was a time when a recoilless gun would have saved many lives, but only the Germans had them.

Three thousand miles away, on the other side of the Atlantic, the United States was in no better shape to start a war than the Europeans had been in 1939. The Depression, inertia, and peace had had the usual effects.

The unready state of the US Army for armoured warfare was clearly shown by a survey in 1941 which discovered the fact that only VI Corps had issued any instructions on anti-tank defence. Wrote General Lesley J. McNair on 12 April 1941:

> It is beyond belief that so little could be done on the question in view of all that has happened and is happening abroad. I for one have missed no opportunity to hammer for something real in the way of anti-tank defence, but so far have gotten nowhere. I have no reason now to feel encouraged, but can only hope that this apathy will not continue indefinitely.

At the time that General McNair was writing, the US Army relied for its defence against tanks upon an inadequate armoury of 37mm infantry guns and the o·5in machine-gun. To back up this thin screen there was the venerable 75mm field gun, appearing in a variety of roles and on several different carriages. The US Army had watched the blitzkrieg roll over the Low Countries and France and during the two summers of 1940 and 1941 various improvised self-propelled guns, or tank destroyers as the Americans preferred to call them, were tried out. It was quickly found that mobility was the key to success with anti-tank guns in a moving war and in late 1941, fifty of the new M2 Half-Track carriers were fitted with 75mm guns and sent to the Philippines where they were just in time for the Japanese invasion.

The M2 Half-Track was to become one of the better-known vehicles of World War II, and certainly as well loved by its crews as was the jeep. With a 75 on board it was up to the limit of its load-carrying capacity, if not a little above it. The gun was mounted by taking the wheels, trail and axle off the field carriage and bolting the remainder to the floor of the Half-Track immediately behind the driver's cab. The barrel of the gun stuck out over the bonnet and the breech recoiled a good distance into the crew compartment. Traverse was limited to 21° either side, and the centre line of the barrel was all but 7ft above ground. Swinging the gun any farther than 21° was liable to lift one set of tracks off the ground; firing broadside there was a distinct danger of inversion. It was not by any means easy to hide, and with only $\frac{1}{4}$in-thick armour it was highly vulnerable to anything except small arms. But it did well against the Japanese and was put into production in time to land in North Africa in large numbers where it proved to be useful, though not entirely a battle-winner. Its chief trouble, apart from its size, was the gun. The ammunition was the same as had been fired in 1918; in fact, much of it was made in 1918, and it lacked the necessary punch to knock out the later German tanks. There was always some uncertainty about the fuze action and by September 1944 the Gun Motor Carriage M3, as it was called, was declared obsolete.

To digress for a moment. The same gun was fitted to the General Grant and Sherman tanks, though the recoil mechanism was altered for the tank turrets, and the limitations on the ammunition became even more apparent. In late 1941 a team was sent up to Syria to retrieve as many French fuzes as could be found and about 60,000 of a 1917 vintage were hauled out of store and taken back to the Suez Canal Zone. Here they were put into the American ammunition and at the same time the opportunity was seized to improve the propellant. Each cartridge case was emptied into a large drum and the old propellant was mixed with an equal proportion of a new and more powerful variety. Hired labourers stirred the mixture until it was reasonably well blended, and it was then poured back into the cases. The resulting brew gave a far better muzzle-velocity than the original and, since the tanks were firing at pretty close ranges, the changes in sight angles were small enough to be easily allowed for. The one allotment of improved ammunition was just enough for the battle of Alamein and, as the tanks chased Rommel along the coast, the supplies ran out and the guns had to revert to the old pattern of round.

A light version of the 75 was made for light tanks, and later in the war it was adapted for aircraft mounting and went into the nose of a Douglas Boston or Martin Maryland for anti-shipping and anti-submarine work. There appear to be no records of this type of 75 ever being used against tanks, though it might well have been useful.

One of the best US guns was the 3in, which came about as a result of a specification in late 1940 for a gun which would stop any tank then known in the world. With no time to design and produce a new gun, the Ordnance Department married up as many existing components as were suitable for the job. The result was the 3in M5, which used an anti-aircraft barrel mounted on the carriage of the 105mm field gun. It was a highly effective gun, but was heavy and clumsy and its fuzes gave continual trouble so that the armour-piercing shell never had the penetration and reliability that was needed. The fuze was not improved until 1944, whereupon the gun began to perform extremely well, but by now it had a bad reputation to live down and there was only a small number of guns in existence. When the shells had given so much trouble, production of the gun was slowed down and by the end of the war the 3in was quite rare. Had a little more effort been put into curing the ammunition troubles, it is quite possible that it would have become one of the better infantry guns of World War II. Certainly the American soldiers would not have been left as vulnerable to tanks as they were.

By 1944 the US Army had produced the 90mm T8 anti-tank

gun, a large and heavy weapon, but a most effective one. This again relied on an anti-aircraft gun for the barrel but this time it was mated to a special carriage designed for the job. It was a good gun but it came too late to see service in any numbers although the 90mm barrel was mounted on a Sherman tank chassis and became the M10 Tank Destroyer. This vehicle was highly successful and became most popular with tank crews who appreciated the power of the 90mm gun. By the time the 90 had appeared the old 75s in the Shermans had become almost a liability, despite an improvement in muzzle-velocity and a lengthening of the barrel and it may be that the infantry version of the 90mm was given lower priority in the rush to give the tank units more fire-power.

However, the American infantry got rather less than they deserved from their gun designers throughout the war and when it became obvious that the 37mm was well out of date – which had happened before Pearl Harbour but was not appreciated by the War Department until some time after – there was no improved gun ready to take its place. The 37 had to make do, and it appeared on a variety of mountings in the hope that more mobility could in some way compensate for a lack of fire-power. It was the same story with all the other small guns in the Allied armies. There were portee versions and half-tracked versions, but nothing could hide the fact that the gun simply wasn't powerful enough for the job it had to do. This was a serious matter for the troops about to go to Europe and the only answer in circumstances like that is to take someone else's design and build it as fast as possible. This is exactly what was done and the gun chosen was the British 6-pounder.

This was soon being turned out from American factories in large numbers as the 57mm M1. It was identical in almost every way to the British gun except for some local variations in the traversing arrangements and a slight swelling at the muzzle. It suffered from being too late and too light and in 1944 the infantry divisions simply left them by the roadside as they advanced across France, for by that time there were so many Allied tanks that the notion became quite strong that there was no need to have guns for local defence – that could always be left to the tanks. It was a philosophy which was very plausible in view of the preponderance of Shermans, but it was a dangerous attitude to adopt and some units regretted it in later actions when the Germans counter-attacked and got well into the infantry areas. But still the view persisted that the best anti-tank weapon was another tank, and for the US Army this held for the next twenty years until the missiles showed that events had overtaken the idea, and perhaps the tank as well. In the interim the recoilless guns held sway, and their story is told in a separate chapter.

The greatest contribution to the science of infantry anti-tank defence – if that is a science – that the United States made in World War II was by inventing and producing the best and most popular of all the one-man anti-tank systems, the Bazooka. The Bazooka became the originator of a whole line of shoulder-controlled rocket launchers of all nationalities and since much legend surrounds its beginnings, it may be as well to clarify the mystery.

A certain Colonel Skinner of the US Army was unusual in that from boyhood he was interested in rockets and built and fired them. In 1931 he transferred to the Ordnance Corps and was posted to Aberdeen Proving Ground where he continued to build and fire small-sized, high-speed rockets in his spare time. By 1938 he had amassed a considerable knowledge on this obscure subject – which interested the Army not at all. He was sent to Hawaii, but was recalled in 1940 and put to work on a 'Special Project', namely, to see if his rockets could be of any use as weapons. With no funds and no support he worked with a staff of one and in less than a year he had produced and tested a simple shoulder-fired rocket, launched from a tube and stabilised by folding fins. All it lacked was a warhead. This came in a dramatic way. In 1940 the Swiss designer of the shaped-charge device which had so signally failed to impress the British attaché arrived in the USA with his secret still intact – as far as the USA was concerned. He managed to sell his idea to the Americans, which must have satisfied him and he forthwith returned to Switzerland. The US promptly put a crash programme into effect to equip the army with hollow-charge grenades. The design chosen was the Grenade, High-Explosive, Anti-Tank M-10, which was excellent in every way except for its weight.

It was too heavy to be projected from the muzzle of a rifle or even a o·50in machine-gun – an idea tried in desperation – and the Ordnance Corps found itself the unhappy owner of a rapidly growing pile of M-10 grenades which nobody wanted to shoot. An experimental grenade-launcher proved to be too big and still with too much recoil. Another idea which only received scant attention was to add a small rocket to the base of the grenade and launch the whole thing from the muzzle of the Springfield rifle, using the long bayonet as a launch rail. The idea takes a lot of beating for ingenuity, but none for common sense since the rocket fired its jet straight back into the face of the firer.

In the spring of 1942 Skinner decided to try and combine the M-10 with his shoulder-launcher. He redesigned his prototype to accept the M-10 and arrived at an internal diameter of 2·36in as being large enough to allow the grenade to move without jamming. A piece of tube was made to this specification and fitted with two hand grips and an electrical firing mechanism using torch batteries. A dozen rockets were made up with dummy heads and three were fired successfully. With the remaining nine Skinner went to Aberdeen Proving Ground to try his idea on a proper range. To his surprise a demonstration was in progress involving a tank being used as a target for some other launching devices for the M-10 grenade. It was an auspicious moment and Skinner and his assistant, Lieutenant Uhl, took post at the end of the line without bothering to tell anyone who they were. The story is now best told in Skinner's own words as given me by Mr Dave Harris of Redstone Arsenal, Alabama:

> It happened that the target tank came up our way to make a turn, and we decided to fire at it. Uhl devised a makeshift sight for the launcher on the spot with a piece of wire he picked off the ground. He hit the tank with his first shot. Then, before it could complete its turn, I hit it with another rocket. By then, partly due to the unfamiliar noise of the rocket blast, the whole multi-starred audience was headed our way. General Barnes (Major-General Barnes of Ground Forces Development) took a shot and made a hit. The other staff people fired until all our rounds were gone. Right there and then the Bazooka was ordered into pilot production design and very shortly after, even before statistical test, into full production.

It was a momentous decision, and a correct one.

On 19 May 1942, the Ordnance Corps contracted with the General Electric Company to make 5,000 Bazookas in thirty days. They did it with eighty-nine minutes to spare. There was then another demonstration firing, this time rather more formally arranged, and scores of high-ranking officers and Allied Representatives watched. This is probably the point at which the Soviets first learned of the weapon because they asked for it immediately afterwards and several hundred of the first production batch were sent to Russia where they were straightaway committed to battle – and captured by the Germans. Another large production order followed this second demonstration and most of it went direct from the factories to ships loading for the North Africa invasion. Some were actually flown to the ports to catch the ships before they sailed, and for 1942 this was pretty remarkable. The result was that the first troops to take the Bazooka into action did so with very little training, but even so they performed amazingly well. One of the first combat reports from North Africa told of a detachment of German tanks which surrendered after several rockets scored near misses at extreme range (obviously the gunners were nervous and firing too soon). On being interrogated the tank commander told his captors that he thought himself to be under fire from 105mm howitzers and as a result it was foolish to go on fighting. The Germans called it at first the 'shoulder 75mm'. The GIs were more prosaic and dubbed it 'the Buck Roger's gun' until some genius jokingly referred to the awkward tube as a 'Bazooka', after the name given to a home-made trombone played by the radio comedian of the era, one Bob Burns. The name stuck and became famous.

The US Army Ordnance Department quickly saw that although the Bazooka was a marvellous invention, it was too small and would soon be out of date on the battlefield. They designed and built a bigger and more effective model which was 3·5in in tube diameter but the War Department would have none of it and the design was shelved despite the evidence of successful firings. The Bazooka continued in service with its 3½lb rocket and its muzzle-velocity of 300ft per second and sure enough, exactly as the Ordnance Department prophesied, by 1945 it was proving to be too small and too weak for the last versions of the German tanks.

There is one interesting story about the Bazooka which is little known now. In 1944, during the sticky infantry fighting around the northern France bridgeheads, a certain sergeant hit upon a field expedient for producing a more effective grenade-thrower. He unscrewed the warhead from a Bazooka projectile and in its place fitted on two standard US hand-grenades, in tandem. The attachment must have been very crude, but it worked. The loader pulled out the pins on the grenades as he gingerly inserted them into the breech of the launcher, the firer shot them off, and four seconds later there was a most satisfying explosion accompanied by a shower of shrapnel. Picatinny Arsenal was persuaded to make up 90,000 of these projectiles, which it did – under protest – and they were rushed to France. By that time the battle had moved away from the hedgerows and ditches of the Bocage and the need was less urgent. No more were ever made and now only one remains in the small museum of the Arsenal as mute evidence of the ingenuity of one man under the stress of battle.

There were other improvements to the basic Bazooka, the most satisfactory being the substitution of an electric generator in the trigger mechanism in place of the torch batteries which the first models used. Later models had an optical sight and a launch tube which could be broken in two parts for easy carriage. In one form or other the Bazooka survived the war and soldiered on into the first actions in Korea in the summer of 1950. There it lost its reputation. Through a combination of bad ammunition and bad training it failed to stop the North Korean tanks in their first push down to Pusan and reports bordering on the limit of panic were flashed back to the USA. The Ordnance Department, remembering the 3·5in improved Bazooka of 1943–4, sent for the drawings and ordered it into production without delay. Within a very few weeks, thousands of the new launchers and rockets were being flown from factories all over the USA to the western seaboard to be loaded into ships and rushed to Korea. A few were even flown all the way so that men could be trained to use the new weapon before the ships arrived. Luckily the

3·5in came up to expectations and was so successful that it remained in service with the regular US Army until only a short
while ago and is still to be found in the National Guard. It sold
well to other countries and was for many years the mainstay of
the NATO short-range infantry anti-tank defence until being
superseded by more modern weapons. It is a remarkable history,
started by two devoted men and helped by a fortuitous demonstration to an unexpectedly high-ranking audience.

By and large the US anti-tank story in World War II was
undistinguished except for the astonishing Bazooka. In the
medium- and large-gun field the US Army was not well served
by its designers and factories, and to have to rely on an outdated
foreign field gun for its main tank armament and chief anti-tank
gun for most of the war was little short of ludicrous. Apart from
the Bazooka the infantry had few effective weapons with which
to defend themselves and so the doctrine grew up that the best
anti-tank defence is another tank; but the fallacy of this was
seen as early as July 1941 when General McNair in another
of his prescient statements said, 'It is poor economy to use a
$35,000 tank to destroy another tank when the job can be done
by a gun costing a fraction as much.' However, at that time the
US had plenty of tanks.

In the post-Korean War years the US infantry held on to the
3·5in rocket-launcher until it was well out of date and overdue
for replacement. In the early 1960s there appeared another
remarkable American anti-tank invention, one that was as novel
and as revolutionary as the Bazooka had been twenty years before.
This was the M-72, the throw-away rocket-launcher. There was
nothing new in the throw-away idea – it had first been pioneered
by the Panzerfaust – but the M-72 goes a step farther: it is a
prepackaged round of ammunition which is waterproof, reliable,
and to some extent 'soldier-proof'. A man carries one of these
until he needs to fire it, he then opens it up, fires and leaves
the empty launch tube on the ground. For his next shot he
collects another complete M-72. This extraordinary little weapon
is a two-part launch tube, in which one half telescopes into the
other. Inside is the rocket, ready to fire. Outside are simple
folding sights and a cocking mechanism. The ends of the tube

are closed by lids which also hold the ends of the carrying sling. Complete, the weight is 5½lb or roughly the same as three hand-grenades. To bring the weapon into action, the lids are flipped off and discarded, along with the sling. The tube is then pulled out to its full length which is 27in. As this is done, the sights pop up and the action is cocked. A safety catch is pulled out and the weapon is ready to fire. The firer puts the tube over his right shoulder, looks through the sights and fires by squeezing a button on top of the tube. There are neither pistol grips nor a trigger.

The rocket is quite small, 66mm in diameter, so that it does not have a dramatically destructive effect upon a tank but, with a hit in the right place, even the largest fighting vehicle can be knocked out, and against armoured cars and light tanks it can be devastating. In Vietnam it proved to be deadly against the Soviet PT-76, if the weapon was handled by determined men. The range is naturally short, about 150yd, but one could hardly expect more from something so small and light. It is now in service with several NATO countries where it has been enthusiastically received and it seems to be the perfect weapon for airborne forces, special forces and citizen volunteer militias.

5

THE EASTERN
INFLUENCE

Never trust the Tartars . . .

Tsi Hung Chi, 112 BC

During World War II the Allies all used US or British equipment except for Soviet Russia which designed and produced its own, although gratefully accepting whatever the others could spare and often giving few thanks in return.

Russia entered the war in a worse state of preparation than her allies, if such a thing can be possible. Lulled by the success of Soviet tanks in the Winter War against the almost unprotected Finns, very little serious thought was given to a family of anti-tank weapons and the infantry found itself facing the German blitzkrieg with a 45mm gun which was no more than a scaled-up 37mm and very little more effective. It was good enough against some of the older German tanks, but as a weapon of war it was antiquated even by 1941 standards and it had to be quickly phased out, a process that was simplified by the large numbers captured in the German advances during that summer. Its replacement was a 57mm, no great advance either and already out of date by the time it reached the troops in 1942, though very useful when several were used together against a small number of tanks. But the increase in calibre from 45mm to 57mm was nowhere near enough to keep up with the improvements in tanks – or for that matter to even catch up with those which had not been improved at all. But rather than try to produce yet another generation of anti-tank gun, the Russians took a step back to

The modern rifle-launched grenade from FN of Belgium. This specimen has been sectioned to show the small hollow-charge explosive content.

Page 107 Two anti-tank grenades: Soviet hand-thrown RPG-43 of World War II. The conical cover dropped off on throwing and allowed a steadying cloth streamer to trail behind.

Page 108 (*above*) Wombat firing at night. A dramatic photograph which exaggerates the size of the back-blast because of the time exposure used. However, the proportion between muzzle and back flash is obvious; (*below*) The Krupp 75mm recoilless gun of 1943. In this photograph the barrel has been tilted forward for loading. The gun saw service in small numbers for a short time.

1917 and made all field guns have a secondary role of destroying tanks. This simplified the production problem, which was formidable, and it ensured that the anti-tank guns were always big enough to be able to cope with the tanks. As with everything so apparently simple, there were snags. The guns were not under control of the infantry, who could not therefore site them in the places where they wanted them, but in compensation the infantry did not have to move them, and perhaps the one outweighed the other. The Soviet factories were able to turn out enormous quantities of guns and there never seemed to be a shortage after the disasters of 1941 had been overcome.

The first encounters with the Wehrmacht had been more than distressing for the Russians and the shortcomings of their anti-tank defences were made very plain. The city of Tula was only saved from capture in October 1941 by a regiment of 85mm anti-aircraft guns which, taking a leaf out of the 88mm book, were deployed in an anti-tank position in front of the city and knocked out twenty German tanks in as many minutes. It was not long before the 85mm gun was to appear as a field/anti-tank gun as well as a tank gun on the T-34. It was supremely successful in both these tasks and is still in service in some of the Satellite countries though it must be relegated to the reserve forces by now. The Russians never tried to use the 85mm on its AA mounting as the Germans did with the 88mm, and it always appeared in the field on a conventional split-trail carriage with a small shield. By 1944 the 85mm was supported by a 100mm gun, and again this one still survives in several countries. When it appeared, it was not only used as a field/anti-tank gun but was also fitted into tanks and put on to a self-propelled chassis and called an assault gun. It was the same with all the other guns which were produced. They grew in size until one marvels that they could ever be dug in and concealed and they were moved by large tractors with big crews. On the Steppes it was a matter of strength rather than guile which won the day and the Germans were in the end overwhelmed by sheer mass.

For the close defence of their infantry the Soviets showed less concern or effort. Two or three different brands of hollow-charge grenade were issued in quantity and it was assumed that the necessary courage and recklessness would be forthcoming for their proper use. It usually was, but it is surprising to find these grenades still in service today; yet more than one reliable source of information on Soviet armaments continues to show them as being in service with the infantry, and in Vietnam they were used by the Viet-Cong on many occasions.

The other weapon peculiar to the Soviet infantry was the anti-tank rifle. There were two models, the PTRD and PTRS, both introduced in 1941 and both firing the heavy 14·5mm round. The introduction of these two roughly coincided with the fading-out of such weapons in other armies, but they survived with the Russians throughout the war. The only possible reason can be that there was no other design available and the factories were full to capacity making the more important guns and tanks. If true, this is a good reason; but one would like to know why the US Bazooka was not copied – perhaps it was factory space again for the Soviets knew how to make hollow-charge projectiles. We shall probably never know for the Soviets are not interested in helping military historians.

The PTRD was an unusual rifle in that it was composed of the absolute irreducible minimum required to make it work at all. On first sight one is struck by the incredibly long barrel, and the fact that the rest of the gun looks as if it is a collection of bits on the barrel, an impression which is not far wrong. The receiver is a short tube screwed on to the breech with a minimal stock, pistol grip and cheek piece dangling from the rear end of it. A carrying handle is clipped to the barrel with a bipod just in front of it. At the muzzle is a large square muzzle brake and a fore-sight. Apart from the bolt and a backsight that is all. The only non-metal parts are the two pieces of wood either side of the carrying handle, two more on the pistol grip and a piece of padded canvas laced to the shoulder plate. But there was a little more to the PTRD than met the eye. The minuscule stock contained a spring and telescoped to absorb the recoil; to the non-moving part was screwed a small wedge-shaped plate which acted as a cam and opened the bolt as it recoiled backwards. This action extracted the fired case and ejected it; the only action required of the gunner to reload was to take another round and feed it into the breech via a cut in the top of the tubular bolt-way. He then slammed the bolt shut. It is very simple and easy, but without the automatic opening of the bolt it would be hard work to rotate the handle and pull out the fired case. The firer's face is protected from the mechanism by another flat plate, this one on the left side.

Despite its simplicity the gun is quite heavy, 38lb, and inordinately long at 79in. Its stablemate was the PTRS 41 which was a semi-automatic rifle very similar to the PTRD but from another designer, this time Simonov. It fired the same ammunition and worked by a simple gas system in which a bolt-carrier was moved by a piston to work the bolt in the usual fashion and feed the rounds on the return stroke from a magazine underneath. Although it should have been a much better weapon, the PTRS was always too flimsy and suffered from frequent failures in the mechanism. Even so, it weighed 46lb and was 84in long – or exactly 7ft. It suffered because of the attempt to fire too powerful a cartridge from too light a weapon; the 20mm guns built in other countries were twice as heavy and as result could stand up to the battering of high-powered ammunition. The PTRS tried to remain a one-man weapon system and it could not do it. Nevertheless, both it and the PTRD stayed in service in the Soviet Army until 1945 and thereafter the PTRD was frequently seen in the equipment of Satellite countries. In Korea a few, fitted with a telescopic sight, were used by the North Koreans as sniping rifles. The accurate range was about 1,500m, with a considerable punch still in the bullet at the end of the flight. Others remained for years with the smaller countries as infantry anti-tank weapons and a reliable source affirms that two years ago it was still to be found with the Albanian Army in first-line service.

The 14·5mm round of ammunition remains in service in the KPV heavy machine-gun which is carried on Soviet armoured personnel carriers and some tanks. It is also used as a low-level, anti-aircraft gun in both twin and quadruple mountings. The KPV is one of the most powerful machine-guns in the world at the moment, rivalled only by the many 20mm models, which are all larger and heavier.

Like the British and Germans, the Russians tried aircraft mountings for anti-tank weapons. Their first efforts were confined to bombs and dive-bombing attacks with the IL-2 Stormovik. These were not entirely successful and a rocket-assisted bomb was tried. Originally this was intended for the attack of fortifications, but it had some success against tanks. The difficulty, as always, was to get a hit; once the tank was hit, there was no doubt about its being knocked out. Luckily the IL-2 was a robust and well-armoured plane which could withstand an enormous amount of fire from small arms and light AA weapons and it was decided to try it with a pair of big guns in the same way as the Stuka. The Soviets had a 37mm AA gun in service which was a pre-war Bofors design. In the AA role it was fed from six-round clips but for aerial use it was modified to belt feed. This modification apparently took all of eighteen months to complete, which seems a very long time and the gun-carrying Stormovik did not come into service until the early months of 1945, by which time the urgency for its use had declined. The IL-2 did not take kindly to the mounting of two guns. Each was fed by a belt whose capacity varied from fifty-five to eighty rounds, depending upon the mission and the amount of fuel required. The load of guns and ammunition was considerable and made the plane sluggish and heavy to fly. When they fired, the machine yawed and swayed, upsetting the aim. The pilots disliked the arrangement and it did not survive for long.

After 1945 there was in Russia the same pause in the development of weapons as happened in other countries. In the 1950s there appeared the first of the Soviet shoulder-controlled rocket-launchers, the RPG-2. This weapon was a cross between a Bazooka and a Panzerfaust. The warhead hung out of the front of the launch tube in the same way as the Panzerfaust, but the propulsion was by rocket and the tube was held over the shoulder like the Bazooka. At the time it appeared, the RPG-2 warhead was quite good although the effective accurate range was little better than that of the wartime Bazooka and its derivatives. Most of the Satellite countries adopted the RPG, many of them modifying the design slightly and building their own versions. It is still in service in some countries and was used by the Viet-

Cong against US vehicles, though with little success against armour since it no longer has a good enough warhead for modern tanks. Its successor is the RPG-7, a much more powerful weapon. Externally there is not a great deal of difference between the 2 and the 7. Both have a short launch tube with the warhead of the projectile sticking out in front, are fired from the shoulder, and use a small optical sight. But the RPG-7 has several significant improvements. The back of the tube is flared into a cone shape and the projectile has small rocket nozzles in the back part of the warhead, the nozzles pointing backwards of course. When the projectile is in its launch tube, these nozzles are just clear of the mouth of the tube, so that in fact they point back into the firer's face. The projectile is fired out of the tube by a recoilless gun charge; this starts off the flight but is not enough to carry it for very far. When the projectile is well clear of the launch tube, the rocket lights up and continues to push the projectile at the same speed. It may even accelerate it.

This apparently complicated propulsion arrangement is extremely successful and has several advantages. Firstly it allows the rearward blast on launching to be reasonably small, and therefore easily concealed. Secondly it offers a flat trajectory for the projectile which simplifies the gunner's job. The range of the 7 is apparently greater than many other similar weapons and the warhead is particularly effective, as the Israelis found to their cost in the 1973 October War. The actual penetration of the RPG-7 is a close secret, but it seems that the Soviets have fitted a very powerful hollow charge inside the comparatively small space of the rocket head, and this charge is well able to knock out a tank. Once again it seems that the single infantryman crouching in his foxhole may have caught up with the tank; it will be interesting to see for how long he remains ahead.

The Japanese were as alert to the danger of tanks as anyone, perhaps a little more so since they had carefully watched the European nations and followed their lead. In addition there was the 'China Incident' which gave them some slight experience in anti-tank warfare. But like all the rest, Japan entered the war relying on two main weapons, an infantry rifle and a light gun. The rifle was a good one, unlike the initial models in Western countries. It was the Model 97, a 20mm automatic rifle and the nearest that the Japanese came to originality in weapon design until recent years. The basic design was intended for AA or anti-tank use, but the two purposes required slightly different characteristics and only the ammunition was standardised in the end. It operated by gas and blowback, was fed by a magazine of twenty rounds and was air-cooled. There was the usual bipod and, to help the small-sized Japanese soldier, there was also a monopod under the butt. This certainly made it an easy gun to hold and aim, but almost entirely prevented any chance of traversing with a moving target. The ammunition was not particularly powerful, and one source quotes a penetration of $\frac{1}{2}$in at 200yd, which seems low for the calibre. Firing the rifle was not unpleasant and one man who fired many rounds through captured guns says that the recoil was very moderate, but when firing automatic there was a good deal of movement which threw the aim off entirely and, in any case, the target was obscured by the muzzle smoke.

The rifle weighed 152lb with a full magazine, making it the heaviest one of its class ever to be built. The crew carried it by two special carrying handles, shaped like a larger version of bicycle racing handlebars, giving two hand grips at front and rear. An unusual feature of this rifle was that it fired automatic only. This was a direct inheritance from the AA requirement and, to simplify manufacture, no single-shot capability was put into the anti-tank version. Accounts of its use and effectiveness are very hard to come by and one is forced to conclude that it saw little action in its proper role.

The complementary weapon to the Model 97 was the Model 34 (1934) 37mm infantry gun. This was intended as a general support and anti-tank gun. It could be pack-carried, towed by a vehicle, or by horses. The specifications were rather out of date by 1941 but it was still a useful weapon. It was part of the equipment of the infantry battalion and remained in service throughout the war, although it was less frequently met in the latter stages when the Japanese had almost no vehicles or horses for towing it. The barrel could be traversed through 60° and, to give the gunner more room on the left-hand side, the left wheel could be slewed outwards 45° without taking it off its axle. Apart from this novelty it differed little from all the other 37mm guns except that it had a muzzle-velocity of 2,400ft per second, which put it among the leaders in that field. It lasted the war, not because there were any better guns to replace it, but because there were not enough better guns and deficient or not the 37 had to stay in action.

The companion weapon to the Model 34 was the Model 1 47mm gun which appeared in late 1941. The Model 1 was an up-to-date design for its time and quite effective for its size. Its drawback was that it was too small on the day that it was first issued, but that was not yet realised by the Japanese and in the 1941–2 campaigns nothing happened to give any cause for disquiet about it. Later on, when the Shermans started storming ashore on the island beaches, it was a different matter. The Model 1 was a 6-pounder, firing a shell which was within ounces of that weight; it had a long barrel and even longer trail legs. The carriage was low-set and the wheels wide apart. It had excellent stability, and it needed to have because there was no muzzle brake. Why the Japanese never fitted one is a mystery because a properly designed muzzle brake can cut down the recoil of the barrel by as much as 25 per cent; with a good muzzle brake the gun could either have been made lighter and smaller or it could have been given a higher muzzle-velocity on the existing chassis. However, brake or no brake, it was quite a good weapon of its class with a muzzle velocity of 2,700ft per second and a good rate of fire owing to its semi-automatic, horizontal sliding-block breech and light ammunition.

In the Japanese infantry division each regiment had an anti-tank company ostensibly armed with 47mm guns, but all too often there were only 37mm ones available. The number of guns varied according to the theatre of operations and the role of the regiment but the standard size was six – occasionally it was four. The division also had an independent anti-tank battalion under its command and this was expected to have eighteen guns in three companies of six. Later in the war, as guns and manpower became scarcer, the independent battalions became independent companies with eight guns each. Each regiment also had some organic artillery in the shape of 75mm field guns. These guns came in several different models, all firing roughly the same ammunition. There was an anti-tank shell for every type of gun and on occasions these guns were wheeled up into the infantry areas and used for close anti-tank defence. They were quite formidable in this role except that they were difficult to hide and, once they were knocked out, the regiment had also lost its support artillery.

When the US began to put armoured forces ashore to support the amphibious assaults on the Pacific islands, the defects of the Model 1 became all too clear and a larger gun was called for. It appeared right at the end of the war and was the best that the Japanese ever made. This was the 75mm M 90. It was capable of penetrating the armour of a Sherman at a thousand yards and the few that were deployed in the islands did good work before they were knocked out. It closely resembled the Model 1 in general features, although it was proportionately higher from the ground owing to a different and rather complicated springing system. The gun was so good that attempts were made to put it into tanks, but the turrets could not be adapted to take it and the idea had to be dropped. In the end an SP gun was built to take the gun, but it was by now too late, and few, if any, were in the hands of the troops by the time of VJ-Day. One curious feature of this otherwise very modern gun was the fact that two of the crew members travelled in seats on the front of the shield, facing backwards. This is almost an archaic way of carrying gunners, which has been out of use in Western countries since the end of World War I, yet it survived on the M 90.

There were no other specific anti-tank weapons in the Japanese armoury, although there were plenty of make-shifts. All manner of AA guns were pressed into service for repelling tanks as the need arose, and on at least one occasion 20mm guns were taken out of shot-down aircraft and mounted on crude wooden trolleys and used to repel attacks on an airfield. But for the infantry in their foxholes there was little that was effective. A magnetic mine was produced in 1940 which would cling to any part of a tank and provided that one accepts that throwing mines on to tanks is a good way of knocking them out – this author does not so think – then a magnetic one is worthwhile. Later on, by about 1943, other and cruder hand-thrown devices appeared. One was a conical-shaped explosive charge standing on a wooden base and enclosed in a silk bag. A cone was made in the explosive to give a hollow-charge effect and a simple fuze activated on impact. The effective range was quoted as 10yd or less, which would not only make sure of the tank but would positively ensure the end of the thrower at the same time. There were also copies of the German Scheissbecher rifle grenades, but these were virtually useless except against light armour.

The Japanese did not have undue confidence in conventional anti-tank measures and placed great emphasis on tank-hunting parties. These were generally specially trained and were attached to each infantry platoon actually in combat. The tank hunters were expert at infiltrating into Allied lines, particularly into the tank night laagers. They also ambushed slow-moving tanks or those which had outdistanced their infantry, more particularly at such points as fords or cross-roads. As a rule they went for the command tanks if they could recognise them. Tank-hunting was worked out as a drill; for instance, No 1 might throw a mine under the tracks while No 2 diverted attention from him by throwing phosphorous grenades on to the engine decking. Other, and less sophisticated, devices were mines that were pushed underneath tanks by a soldier lying in a slit trench alongside the road and using a long pole to do the pushing.

On Okinawa at least one Japanese infantry company was only armed with satchel charges. Infantry also rode on tanks and dismounted when close to the Allied anti-tank guns and attacked them with grenades, or cleared minefields under cover of the tank fire, or went forward to attack the Allied tanks in their defensive positions. Any Allied tank commander who put his head out of his turret was running the risk of being shot by a sniper specially detailed for that job.

A particularly crude device was the Lunge mine. This was nothing more than a large conical-shaped mass of explosive on the end of a 6ft pole. The pole fitted into a sleeve on the top of the mine and had a spike in its end. In the mine was a detonator placed so that if the pole travelled more than 2in down the sleeve, the spike crushed the detonator. A safety pin held the two apart until a tank was attacked. The base of the conical charge had three legs projecting so that a reasonable 'stand-off' was achieved. The method of use was both simple and desperate. When a tank was a few yards away from the operator, he withdrew the safety pin, stood up and rushed the tank lunging at it with his mine as if making a bayonet attack. The resulting explosion would virtually destroy a Sherman and unfailingly blow the operator into small pieces. The Shermans quickly learned never to move without infantry round them.

Another Japanese speciality, found only in Burma, was a form of command-detonated mine. When the Fourteenth Army came down into the plains of Burma in 1944 and started to push the Japanese back to Rangoon, it met a novel form of anti-tank weapon. It was found that holes had been dug in the middle of the roads and tracks and the openings carefully and expertly camouflaged. In each hole was a large artillery shell, nose upwards, and in some an aircraft bomb. In the nose of each was a detonator and sitting cuddling the shell, holding a hammer, was a Japanese soldier waiting for a tank to run over his hide-out so that he could blow it up straight through the belly-plates. There are other recorded instances of soldiers strapping mines to their backs and crawling under tanks, or throwing themselves under moving ones, and pulling the initiating cord when squarely under the middle. On one occasion a Japanese officer actually charged a tank with his sword and inflicted considerable personal injuries on the crew before he was killed.

For the Japanese, fighting tanks was an unprofitable and expensive operation. Unlike the Russians they never had enough equipment and what they did have was largely ineffective. The desperate suicide measures that the Japanese infantry was forced to use could only work against the comparatively few tanks that were in the Pacific Theatre. Had the Allies been able to use armour on a European scale, there would not have been much to stop them.

For the Russians it was different. They faced massive and skilful tank attacks; they responded by abandoning finesse and variety and concentrating on the volume production of simple, powerful guns. In the end it worked, and the Panzers were overwhelmed.

6

POST-WAR
DEVELOPMENTS

They shall beat their swords into ploughshares, and their spears into
pruning hooks . . .

Isaiah 2:4

There was little evidence of ploughshare-beating or pruning-
hook manufacture after 1945. Most nations in the world did their
best to retain as strong an army as they could and, whilst few
advances were made in equipment, at least the 1945 models
were allowed to remain in service. This state of affairs continued
with little change until the Korean War, whereupon there was
a marked change in thinking. For one thing, the war emphasised
that research must go on; and for another, it brought out the
deficiencies in much of the old World War II equipment. This
was nowhere more true than in anti-tank weapons, and the
Americans were lucky to have had the 3·5in rocket-launcher in
such a state of readiness that they could make it without pausing
to check the design in any way. After 1954 there was also a noticeable stirring among the NATO nations in the direction of better
close-range weaponry, and this coincided also with the first anti-
tank, guided-missile designs.

The US 3·5in rocket-launcher became the staple short-range
weapon of the NATO armies, its popularity, to some extent at
least, being based on the effectiveness of the wartime Bazooka
rather than the actual battle record of the 3·5in itself. In fact the
3·5 and many of the other rocket-launchers were and still are
called bazookas, a generic term which is not generally accepted

in military terminology. Thousands of 3·5in launchers still exist in many countries of the world, though the situation of the ammunition supply must by now be a little difficult, for the launcher is a very secondary part of any rocket system. It is the ammunition, or in other words the rocket, which determines the success or failure of the whole thing.

An anti-tank rocket-launcher has only to guide the rocket on the start of its flight; it takes no firing stresses nor strains nor does it have to impart a twist to the projectile. It can be made of any material that does not actually burst into flame when the rocket passes close to it and which is strong enough to support the rocket while it travels up the tube. It could almost be compressed paper, but it has to be stronger than that because of one potent feature of military life, the soldier's boot. A paper tube would last two minutes or less in action before it became crushed out of shape, so the rocket-launcher tube is made of metal of a gauge sufficiently tough to stand up to rough treatment, and that puts the weight up. The ends of the tube are more vulnerable than the middle and for this reason the second version of the original Bazooka was given a bell mouth at the muzzle and a wire frame round the breech end. These additions reduced the dangers of distortion, and have been copied in many subsequent designs.

The firer is in a highly vulnerable position when he fires the rocket because he has the launcher over his shoulder and his face just alongside the tube. It is most necessary that the rocket shall not be throwing any flame back when it leaves the tube, and much effort goes into ensuring that this never happens. Anti-tank rockets burn up their motors while they are in the tube and this is done so quickly that it produces an almost instantaneous explosion very similar to a gun going off, the rocket then flies out of the tube in much the same way as any other fin-stabilised projectile and away down the range. There is no trail of sparks, as with a toy rocket, but there is a back-blast which blows out of the back of the tube for several yards and is usually cited by the opponents of rocket launchers as being a serious difficulty in camouflaging the firing position. In point of fact this is only partly true because the back-blast is over in a very few thousandths of a second and is easily missed in battle. The one objectionable feature of the rocket-launcher which can neither be avoided nor minimised is the low muzzle-velocity, and this is serious. Most shoulder-launchers have a velocity at launch of less than 500ft per second, which allows only a very short effective range, usually little more than 100yd. Above that range the rocket has to be flying in such a curving trajectory that unless the gunner knows the distance to the target very precisely he is never going to hit it; also of course, if the target is moving, he will have to make such a large allowance for movement that he will again be lucky to hit and a combination of unknown range and moving target will defeat him every time.

Rocket-launchers are essentially single-shot weapons and from time to time there have been attempts to provide some sort of repeating mechanism, or auto-loaders. The idea is not very practicable in view of the size and weight of the ammunition, but every now and then another project appears. It all started in World War II when certain enterprising spirits in the US Army mounted Bazookas in pairs so that they had a second-shot capability and so a better chance of one hit. This was expanded a little in the Korean War when local initiative produced a four-barrelled 3·5in. These clumsy devices were not intended for anti-tank use. They were specifically local close-support artillery for the platoons which owned them and they only ever fired at Chinese trenches. However, the idea stuck and shortly after the war ended Picatinny Arsenal began experimenting with a three-shot repeater 3·5in rocket-launcher.

This novel arrangement used a box magazine on top of the normal tube and the rockets were held in the magazine by spring-loaded fingers. When the bottom one was fired, the gunner turned a crank handle on the front of the magazine and another rocket dropped down into the tube. There were electrical contacts in the sides of the tube which touched the rocket contacts so that it was not necessary to connect up the earth wire – as it was with the normal launcher – and firing could be as fast as the gunner could turn the crank. Unfortunately there were some difficulties. The worst one was a regrettable tendency to explode. This was caused by the flame from the rocket which was being fired entering the magazine and igniting the next one to be loaded. The magazine system depended upon a simple gravity feed and there was no cover between magazine and tube. Although practically all the blast went out of the back of the tube, just sufficient went up the rear wall of the magazine to ignite the next rocket motor, though this did not happen on every occasion. When it did, the resulting fireworks were interesting. Although ingenious (and to some extent ingenuous also) the repeating rocket-launcher is not really a practical weapon of war. Weight and bulk rule it out before it ever really starts and no matter how much one may want a second or third shot, a magazine-loading launcher is not the ideal way to set about it.

But despite all the drawbacks, the rocket-launcher offered a promising way to engage tanks and an extraordinary number of largely similar types appeared in service in different armies in the 1950s. The leaders in what soon became a flood of designs were the Belgians with their Blindicide models. These were very simple launchers using a one-piece barrel and a percussion firing mechanism. Unlike the 3·5in (strangely it was never given a name) which had a launch tube which came apart in the middle so that it was a reasonable load to carry, the Blindicides stuck to single tubes, and this meant that they had to be fairly short in relation to the length of the rocket. This, in its turn meant that the possibility of a bit of motor still burning when the rocket left the muzzle was higher, and all the Blindicides were sold with metal face shields. The firing mechanism was interesting. Plainly the designers had little faith in the electrical systems in the Bazooka family and they tried a conventional percussion cap in the base of the propellant tube. When the rocket was loaded, it was located in the 'breech' by a spring clip which ensured that it could not move forward or backward. A long hammer was pivoted outside the tube and cocked by hand; on firing it swung up and hit the cap; when the propellant fired, the hammer was blown back by the blast and recocked for the next shot. Reloading could be very quick with this system and as the hammer did not stay in the blast stream, it did not suffer much from erosion.

The Blindicides were most successful and were offered for sale all over the world, to the chagrin of the British Army which met them in Aden where they formed the mainstay of the terrorists armouries. They came in several calibres, the largest being 100mm, which is about the maximum for a shoulder weapon. Above this size the rocket has to have a large and heavy motor to drive it; this in turn calls for a longer tube and soon the size of weapon that the man has to carry and conceal becomes tactically unacceptable. Even 100mm was more than most were prepared to undertake, and the more popular calibre was the 83mm version.

The French built a series of excellent launchers and rockets with the Strim family, of whom the latest are still in service. The Strim were fairly normal launchers of conventional pattern and the first model was the 1950 73mm. This resembled any other rocket system, but it has now been replaced by a sophisticated and highly lethal 89mm Model F 1. With the F 1 much attention has been paid to streamlining the rocket and gaining the best possible muzzle-velocity. The exact figure is not revealed, but the effective fighting range is 400m, which is very good for a rocket projectile. The rocket itself is shaped much like a slender artillery shell, with a pointed nose. At the base are nine thin fins which pop out as it leaves the muzzle and assist the accuracy by slowly spinning the projectile. The rocket comes in a plastic case which is loaded into the rear of the launcher and discarded after firing. The whole thing represents the epitome of the rocket-launcher of the older conventional pattern, and it is unlikely to be surpassed by any later models. There are now better and easier ways of firing rockets to long ranges as the RPG-7 has shown.

A more recent French design is the APX 80, which is a recoilless gun of only slightly smaller dimensions than the F 1 rocket-launcher, but with 25 per cent better performance. The shell from this weapon is sustained in flight by a small rocket motor, in the same way as is the RPG-7, though the method is not so revolutionary; with the APX 80 the motor exhausts through a venturi in the tail. The 80mm hollow-charge warhead is claimed to penetrate the heaviest tank and the accuracy is said to be good. Here again modern technology is being used to the utmost to squeeze the maximum out of a very small calibre weapon, small that is for anti-tank work, and the ways in which it is done are interesting to examine.

None of these sophisticated rocket-launchers is particularly cheap, nor are they one-man weapons and in an effort to produce a portable device that can be carried and fired by a single infantryman, the French Army has been experimenting with a few very light models. The Type A is made by MAS and is a tiny conventional gun with a throw-away barrel made of wrapped fibreglass. It is fractionally over 15in long and just under 4in in bore. It comes as a complete round of ammunition with a rubber shoulder pad on one end and a muzzle cap on the other. There is an elementary sight in a block on top of the barrel and in the same block is a withdrawal pin which is the trigger. The manufacturers claim a 'useful' range of 50m for this micro-gun and one would agree that this appears to be the maximum that could be expected without damaging the firer's shoulder. It's an interesting idea.

Spain, not being blessed with a large defence budget, has been forced to use simple weaponry for many years now. Her standard infantry anti-tank weapon is a derivative of the 3·5in, known as the Instalaza. The chief difference in the Instalaza seems to lie in an increased muzzle-velocity and range, which points to a redesign of the rocket, and this is probable since the calibre is very slightly larger than in the American original.

One way to overcome the bugbear of estimating the range of distant targets is to use some sort of rangefinder on the sight. It was the Canadians who tried this with a rocket-launcher called the Heller. The first model appeared in 1956 and there were minor improvements until 1961 and the design stayed in service until about 1967. The Heller was a conventional rocket weapon of straightforward design and good performance. The muzzle-velocity was 715ft per second which is among the highest ever achieved. The best fighting range was 300yd and the weapon was very accurate out to 450yd and the developers were content not to be optimistic and to try to claim more. The sight was the heart of the weapon. It contained a coincidence rangefinder working on a 9in base. Nine inches is not enough for great accuracy, but it was more than good enough for a first round hit at 300yd and an 80 per cent chance at 450yd.

The British Army very nearly adopted the Heller, but in the end the Carl Gustav was chosen instead, to the great disappointment of the Canadians. The reasons for the choice are not now clear for the two have an almost equal performance, but perhaps dollar currency restrictions had some influence on it.

Page 125 (above) The unsuccessful Burney recoilless gun of 1945–8. This is the 3·45in infantry gun and the four venturis are well visible; (below) The US 106mm gun mounted on a jeep. Whilst the gunner maintains his lay on the target the loader pushes in a fresh round. The perforated sides of the cartridge case show up well in this picture.

Page 126 (above) The Swedish Carl Gustav recoilless gun in the firing position. The short length of the barrel should be compared with the Blindicide rocket-launcher; (below) The Czech Tarasnice 82mm rocket-launcher on its field carriage. This specimen was captured in the Suez campaign of 1956.

In the Eastern Bloc the Soviet designs have always been the lead for the others to follow and in the 1950s the standard was set by the RPG-2 which was no more than a simple rocket-launcher with a rocket whose warhead was too large for the tube. Almost all the satellite countries built their own versions of this effective but unlovely device. Each put on some little speciality of its own, in some cases an optical sight, in others a different bipod or a different pistol grip, but all stuck to the basic design, and all probably will fire the same ammunition, although this is not entirely clear as a few of the models quote a different tube calibre from the original Soviet one. It is hardly important; one does not expect to have to swap rocket-launcher ammunition between armies. If things have reached the stage where one army is entirely out of ammunition for its rocket-launchers then other, more serious things, will have gone so far wrong that a resupply is not going to cure the situation.

For several years after the war Britain showed little enthusiasm for rocket-launchers, although two interesting designs were put forward in the late 1940s when it became apparent that the Burney 3·45in recoilless shoulder gun was not going to work. Red Planet was a proposal for a 4·5in rocket-launcher to be fired either from a small tripod or from the shoulder. The one remaining photograph leads one to believe that the launch tube would probably have been a little short for the size of the motor and might well have allowed a back-blast in the firer's face. Anyway, it never got beyond the mock-up stage. Red Biddie was the larger brother of Planet, or perhaps one should say sister. The calibre was to be 5in, which is pretty daunting for a shoulder-fired weapon, and the design soon became a recoilless gun. Even so it was obviously too big and like the Planet it too never got beyond being a mock-up. One imagines that these large-calibre weapons were not intended for any great range of engagement; the idea was solely to carry a large-diameter hollow-charge warhead so that there was a good chance of destroying the tank with one strike. Judging from appearances, 200yd would have been the most that they could have been expected to achieve and still give a better-than-even chance of a hit.

Once these two ideas were abandoned Britain took no further steps to produce a native design and adopted the US 3·5in as soon as the Korean War ended.

The second post-war trend in anti-tank weapons was towards rifle grenades, and this marched very much hand-in-hand with the rocket-launchers – in fact it still does. Despite the poor record of small rifle-launched grenades in World War II, so poor in fact that the British Army dropped them altogether in 1945, the idea persisted in some quarters that a few ounces of explosive could still provide a last-ditch defence for an infantryman faced with an oncoming tank. The chief protagonists of this theory were the Belgian firm of Mecar who began marketing their Energa grenade in 1950. In fairness to Mecar it must be said that the Energa was a much better proposition than any that had gone before. There was just over 11oz of explosive in the hollow-charge warhead and it was at least as effective against armour plate as the 3·5in rocket-launcher and far more so than the Bazooka which was still standard equipment in many armies at that time. To fire the grenade, the rifleman fitted a special adaptor in the muzzle of his rifle. This adaptor weighed only a few ounces and it could easily be carried in the pocket; its purpose was to act as the launch spigot for the grenade. A grenade was slipped over the adaptor, a ballistic cartridge loaded into the breech, and the firer was ready. The trouble lay in the sighting and the slow flight. There was a flip-up rear sight on the adaptor which offered a series of holes for different ranges, but the 'foresight' was the curve of the grenade nose and this was imprecise to say the least. Aiming was largely a matter of practice and it was vital to know the range to a very few yards since the grenade flew on a high trajectory and although Mecar claimed that it was accurate out to 125yd, 75yd was as much as most men could manage and 50yd was preferred. Nevertheless, the Energa could penetrate 200mm of armour plate and although as a tank killer it was a weapon of desperation, it could be most effective against lighter armoured vehicles as well as bunkers, trenches and emplacements. Several NATO armies adopted it including the British, who promptly named it the No 94.

The Energa started other manufacturers along the same path and by 1967 there were no less than seven different types of rifle-launched, anti-tank grenades in service with the NATO armies. To trace their respective histories would be extremely tedious; it is sufficient to say that all of them were launched from the rifle in the same way as the Energa and by 1967 many designs of rifle were being made with a grenade spigot integral with the muzzle so that the adaptor could be dispensed with. All these grenades had the same short effective range and all were more-or-less similar in performance against armour. However, there was another trend appearing at about that time and this was a move towards a much smaller anti-armour grenade that was both easier to carry and more accurate in flight. The move towards the small grenades was in keeping with the corresponding movement towards still smaller rifle calibres, such as ·223in and a realisation that infantrymen simply cannot be expected to carry bulky grenades without damaging them.

The smaller rifles pose a considerable problem to the grenade designer since it is imperative that he keeps the recoil to within certain definite limits. The Energa, for instance, when fired from the Belgian FAL rifle gave a recoil almost exactly seven times greater than when the rifle fired a normal bullet. This enormously increased recoil meant that the rifle had to be propped against some support or held with the sling round the body, and such a severe loading would quickly break up the lightweight ·223 rifles now being considered by many European armies, nor is it particularly desirable from the point of view of the firer since it requires constant practice to overcome an understandable feeling of nervousness when pulling the trigger. The smaller the grenade the easier it is to make it strong without extra weight; the Energa had to be carried in a metal container to prevent damage but the small rifle grenades now offered by such firms as FN can be tucked into a pouch without a lot of harm coming to them. The difficulty is to be certain that they give a big enough effect at the target. It has been unkindly said of one such small grenade that it will knock out any tank in the world provided that it hits the commander in the eye.

The day of the rifle-launched grenade is almost certainly well over now and few armies are going to keep them when there are such excellent throw-away rocket-launchers to be had. The US M72 one-shot launcher has a greater range, greater accuracy and a far better warhead than any grenade can ever hope to have and in the face of this, the only possible reason for keeping rifle grenades in service must be their lower cost, although even this can be disputed.

Although everyone tries to keep up with the Joneses these days, there are still some countries who for various reasons, mostly financial, are continuing to use quite elderly equipment. The Molotov Cocktail for instance still has a part to play in stopping armoured vehicles, given the right conditions and simple ingenuity and bravery on the scale of the Spanish Civil War, and can still be used to good effect. In Hungary in the uprising in 1956 Soviet T-34 tanks were put out of action on several occasions by the crudest possible means. The most successful was to set them on fire, or choke their crews by pouring buckets of petrol on to the roof of the tank as it drove down a narrow street and igniting it with either a Molotov or a petrol-soaked rag dropped from another house. Apparently this ancient method of attack was perfectly successful in causing the crews to dismount and be shot by snipers in other buildings. At least two T-34s were put out of action by pouring a large quantity of used sump oil on the surface of a steep cobbled hill in Budapest. The two tanks lost control going down the hill and slid helplessly into houses at the bottom where they were promptly attacked with Molotovs.

Smoke grenades were also used in the Budapest streets to blind the tanks so that they drove into obstacles or buildings and could then be attacked by the waiting Hungarians while they were stuck, or while their turrets were jammed in one direction.

The venerable 106mm RCL has been adopted by a large number of Western nations, just how many is not clear, but at one time or another it has been in the service of practically every NATO nation, almost every South American country, and several in South-East Asia as well. Much ingenuity has been used in mounting it on different vehicles, not always successfully. The French firm of Chennault offered a small two-man armoured vehicle in the middle 1950s, on which a 106 could be mounted. The vehicle was extremely low, less than 3ft high, and the two men normally travelled lying down. It was tracked and apparently quite manoeuvrable, but lacking in power. It also lacked a roof to protect the crew from overhead fire, but these shortcomings apart, it was an interesting concept. The 106 travelled with its barrel lying fore and aft between the two men; to fire, it was jacked up on a pivoting mount and could be traversed through 360°. The idea was that it acted as a fast-moving gun that could be quickly sent to threatened points in a battalion defence line, or could be sent out with a reconnaissance troop to provide useful anti-armour protection. Sadly nobody bought it to try out the concept but it may have prompted the Japanese to try their version of it.

The Japanese vehicle was very similar to the Chennault, low, open, two-man crew – probably underpowered – but it mounted no less than *two* recoilless guns, this time 75mm, not 106. These were on a special hydraulic mounting which could extend them several feet into the air and traversed them by remote control, sighting being by some indeterminate form of periscope. The idea was that the vehicle could remain hidden behind cover and the guns could be run up until they just cleared the crest and fired in perfect safety. The guns could then be run down, stowed, and the vehicle driven away without the enemy having any idea of where the shells came from. James Bond was still in his apprentice school when this one came out or he would have snapped it up at once. Needless to say, nobody else did.

7
THE RECOILLESS STORY

To every action there is an equal and opposite reaction . . .

Isaac Newton

As the reader will be by now well aware, the great difficulty in making an effective conventional anti-tank gun is to devise some way of firing a heavy shot at high velocity without producing too much recoil at the gun. No matter whether it is a small shell travelling at high speed, or a big one at low speed, the recoil of the gun is a definite problem to the designer. The moment a better penetration performance is called for, the strength of the gun has to increase and it is not long before the infantry find themselves with a cuckoo in their nest. The size and weight soon get to be beyond the limits which a gun crew can handle, and like the PAK 40s in Russia in 1942, the crews cannot pull them out of position without mechanical help.

There was nothing new in the idea of a recoilless gun – engineers had been searching for it for centuries – but the need had become acute after the introduction of smokeless powders and the consequent drastic increase in propellant pressures. Apart from such peculiarities as elastic breech linings which a well-known American charlatan proposed – along with several other equally impractical ideas – the only solution seemed to be to put two guns together facing in opposite directions and fire them simultaneously. The recoil of one would then exactly match that of the other and so the contraption would stay still. This was so absurd that it was never considered for an instant, yet it is precisely the way that all present-day recoilless guns work, with modifications naturally. The solution was found in 1910 by an American naval commander, one Davis. He proposed to use one barrel and fire two shots in opposite directions using a single charge of powder. He thus did away with the need for two guns and two breeches. What he did was to combine the barrels into one and to put his two propellant charges back to back in the middle. It was a brilliant inspiration and it worked perfectly from the very beginning. Davis quickly overcame the problem of firing two identical shells by using a charge of buckshot at the rear. By carefully selecting the right weight, he still had no recoil and the buckshot only flew a short distance. However, it was highly unattractive as a ground weapon and Davis turned his thoughts towards the air.

World War I aircraft were too flimsy to accept the recoil of anything larger than machine-guns, and the US Navy tried the Davis gun as an armament for flying boats engaged on anti-submarine patrols. The gun was mounted right in the nose on a flexible mounting and serviced by one gunner. A Lewis gun was attached to the Davis barrel and used for sighting shots. The idea was to shoot downwards and allow the lead shot to fly up over the top wing of the plane. Although quite successful, few were installed. One problem was perhaps the length of barrel, which was nearly 9ft and must have been very difficult to control in the airstream. After a few other tries at air mountings, the Davis gun was allowed to lapse and aircraft armament remained wedded to rifle-calibre weapons.

The story now shifts to Germany in the 1930s where Krupps were trying to find a way to make infantry-support guns that would fire a big shell, yet not weigh very much. The Davis idea was revived and the Krupp engineers reasoned that it did not matter at all what was fired back for the balancing shot – buckshot was one thing, but a mass of gas would do just as well. To give the same momentum the gas would have to travel fast, but that was no great difficulty and could easily be arranged with a nozzle of the right size. Very secret experiments confirmed that this theory was right, although the muzzle-velocity of the shell would not be high. However, this was not important since the shell could be as big as the user was prepared to accept. In fact its size was more likely to be limited by

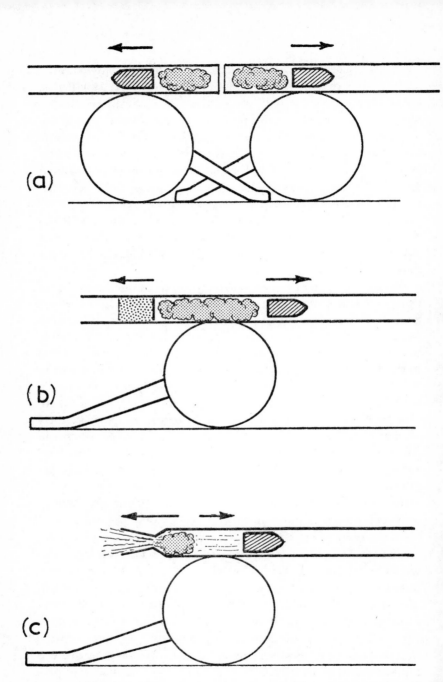

The development of the recoilless gun: (a) the original idea – two guns back to back; (b) the Davis principle – central breech, shell balanced by lead shot; (c) the Krupp principle – shell balanced by mass of gas.

what could be carried rather than by what could be fired.

The attraction of gas was that it could easily be produced by burning propellant, and it was found after some trials that a suitable weight of gas was one-third of that of the shell. In order to balance the momentum the gas was required to travel at three times the muzzle-velocity, but this was not excessive and would not give trouble. Any faster was found to cause wear on the sides of the chamber. To speed up the gas, a choke or venturi was used. This was a restriction in the breech which flared out into a cone-shaped funnel at the rear. The weight of gas was produced by burning the same weight of propellant, so that the cartridge case for a Krupp recoilless gun contained five times as much propellant as did one for a normal gun firing at the same muzzle-velocity. Of these five parts, one pushed the shell forward and one pushed the counter-weight back, so achieving a Davis recoilless effect. Three parts burned up to provide the counter-weight and this was the great breakthrough that the Krupp engineers made, for in a Davis gun three separate items had to be loaded, the shell, the propellant and the counter-weight. In the Krupp gun, only two were needed and these were capable of being loaded in a conventional case just like any other round, albeit rather bigger.

There were two difficulties. Propellant will only burn properly when under pressure and shells are reluctant to start moving. This was overcome by providing an opening in the base of the shell for the counter-weight gas to flow out and then closing it with a bakelite disc. When the gun was fired, the disc held firm and allowed the pressure to build up until the propellant was burning well and until the shell had been given a sufficiently sharp kick to start it on its way up the barrel. The disc then blew out into fine powder fragments that were harmless at a few feet and the gun then began to work on the normal Davis principle: gas one way, shell the other. It is the way every single recoilless gun works today.

Krupps quickly found that it was not necessary to have a central breech as with the Davis gun and the venturi could be put on to the back of a conventional breech block without too much trouble. This was a tremendous advantage since it meant that conventional gun-making techniques could be used and less specialised machinery was needed. They also put the firing cap in the middle

135

of the bursting disc in the same relative place as it is in conventional cartridges and so simplified the ammunition manufacture. Since there was no recoil, the carriage could be light and need carry only the weight of the gun and sighting gear. It was evident from the start that recoilless guns were going to find a ready use with airborne and mountain troops.

The first gun was called the LG 40 (Leicht-Geschoss – light gun), and it was 75mm. It weighed 320lb or about one-sixth of a conventional gun of the same calibre. It had motor-cycle wheels and broke down into four loads so that parachutists could fit it into their containers. It fired a 10lb shell with a hollow-charge head. The hollow charge was quickly to prove a Godsend to the recoilless designers as they could never get enough muzzle-velocity to punch a hole in armour with conventional AP shell, but a hollow charge simply needed to be carried to the target when the explosive did the rest. Another attraction was that hollow-charge shells are light for their size. LG 40 was tried out in the Crete airborne operation and was found to be perfectly satisfactory. It went into limited production as a weapon for airborne and special forces, but as neither of these types of unit was much used after Crete the LG 40 never got a chance to prove itself in its proper environment. Some went to North Africa and a small number were captured by the Eighth Army and sent to the UK and USA where they aroused considerable interest.

In Germany the development of recoilless guns was pursued with some vigour after the partial success of the LG 40 and in quick succession contracts were issued to Krupp and Rheinmetall to develop a 105mm version. Krupp simply scaled up the 75mm but altered the firing mechanism so that it was on top of the sliding breech. On the 75 the firing pin had been housed in a small streamlined block carried on radial arms in the middle of the gas flow. This was necessary because of the central percussion cap; but the flow of fast-moving hot gas soon caused serious wear to the housing, and the firing pin gave trouble. So the 105 put the percussion cap on the side of the case and the firing pin was in the wall of the breech. This left an uninterrupted venturi but meant that the case had to be put into the breech in just the right position, and this was ensured by cutting a notch in the base of the case and providing a key in the side of the chamber to register with it. It slowed down the loading, but not to any great extent. The Rheinmetall 105 was very similar except that it had an even lighter and narrower carriage so that on firing it tended to topple over sideways from the torque effect of the rotating shell. Rather than fit a wider axle, Rheinmetall welded spiral vanes inside the cone of the venturi and this provided sufficient opposite twist to stabilise the gun. Neither of these guns was made in large numbers, and neither was primarily an anti-tank weapon. However, the next one was.

A 75mm anti-tank recoilless gun was ordered and the first version was a failure. Subsequently the LG 40 was improved and became the LG 43, a very much lighter gun altogether with a simple tripod mount and no wheels at all, the total weight without ammunition being only 95lb. It broke down into three loads: barrel, venturi and tripod. To load, the venturi was unlocked from the barrel by rotating and undoing a bayonet joint which joined them. The round was inserted into the exposed breech, and the venturi locked on again. There can be no simpler way of doing it. The firing pin was on the side as in the 105 and the round was indexed to locate it. The first cartridge cases were made of cardboard, but the production model was in plastic, another notable first for the Krupp firm. It does not seem that many of these guns were made, for none were captured in action and in the photographs of remaining models there are no sights to be seen. However, another version did see some war service. This was again a 75mm, again very light, but this time loaded by tipping the barrel forward on its trunnions in the same way that a shot-gun breech is opened. With a shell inserted, the barrel was pushed down to lock on to the venturi. Opening the breech in this way cocked the firing pin just as with a shot gun and the action was both quick and efficient.

These 75mm anti-tank guns were made only in small numbers for the reason that at the same time as they were perfected so were their rivals, the rocket-launchers, and the rocket-launchers used less propellant powder than a gun. From 1943 onwards the supply of powder became critical in Germany, causing the abandoning of several promising designs on the grounds of economy. With the 75s, the 105s went as well, and the German infantry lost what in retrospect looks to have been the best and most worthwhile development series that was ever offered them. A few hundred 105mm anti-tank guns in Russia in 1942 might have made all the difference on the front, and a few hundred more in 1944 might have made the Allied advance across northern France a good deal more expensive than it was.

However, the German faith was partly pinned to another recoilless gun, the Panzerfaust. This has been mentioned already in this book and it only appears here to be examined as an example of the principle. The Panzerfaust was the crudest possible application of a recoilless gun. The propellant charge was black powder contained in a cardboard tube attached to the end of the projectile. The firing tube was a straight-sided pipe with no pretence at a venturi or a blow-out disc. There was no attempt at reloading and, after firing, the gunner threw his tube down and made his retreat. On firing there was a good deal of flame and smoke, particularly to the rear and the projectile, at a very slow speed, wobbled its way to the target in a high curve. Despite all its drawbacks, it worked and it was produced in large numbers. One point in its favour was that it used few scarce materials.

In Britain the development of recoilless guns was in the hands of one man for almost all the war. This was Sir Dennis Burney, a man of enormous talent and a long history of invention and innovation ranging from airships to motor cars. Quite early in the war he saw that the only answer for anti-tank guns was to find some formula for reducing the recoil and he followed the Davis principle on his own to come to the same conclusions as had the Krupp designers. He then built his first recoilless gun using a 4-bore duck gun and leading the gases to the rear with a simple pipe welded to the side of the breech. This worked, and from then on Burney successively improved and enlarged the system, always sticking to the principle of leaving the breech-closing device intact and taking the gas from the side of the chamber and round a corner to the rear. He maintained that in so doing he was simplifying manufacture as the general design of the gun did not need to be altered at all: it was simply necessary to add the venturis at the side of the chamber. This was true enough, but it nullified the great advantage of the recoilless gun which is lightweight. In the end, all of Burney's

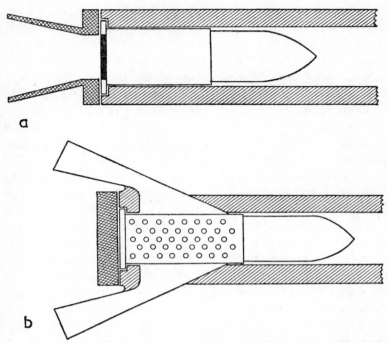

a Single venturi: plastic blow-out disc in base of case; ignition can
be either in the centre of the blow-out disc or in the side of the
case.

b Multi-venturi: normal central ignition in base of case. Holes in
case to allow gas to escape.

guns had to be specially made and so his argument was defeated.

His first practical weapon was a 20mm single-shot gun with the
remarkably high muzzle-velocity of 2,850ft per second. It was
meant for anti-tank use, but this was now 1942 and 20mm guns
had long since ceased to have any value against tanks. The next
development was a repeating version of the single shot, and this
might have had some purpose, but it was never followed up by the
War Office and Burney turned to field guns and howitzers for a
couple of years, coming back in 1944 with the first of two practical
anti-tank designs which caught the imagination of the War
Office and which he was allowed to develop. This was a shoulder-
fired gun of 3·45in – exactly the same as the 25-pounder and also

the 88mm. It is a curious thing how similar calibres crop up all over the world for no apparent reason. This weapon weighed 75lb without its shell, and that added a further 16lb so that the man who fired it was no milksop. The barrel was nearly 5ft long and it was not easy to balance on the shoulder. Had it gone into production, it is certain that it would have been mounted on a tripod.

There were four venturis, or jets as Burney called them, leading out from the chamber. The cartridge case, as with all multi-jet designs, had holes in its sides to allow the gas to escape. The initial pressure was built up by lining the inside of the case with thin sheet brass and allowing it to burst out through the holes. The principle is still used today. Apart from the holes, the shell case was perfectly normal, with the primer in the middle of the base and the same gauges of brass as for a conventional gun. This was an important point in Burney's favour since it required little alteration to existing machines to make the ammunition. It was claimed that the side venturis were safer since none of the brass blew back whereas bits of plastic could and did fly back from the centre-venturi models. But this was nonsense, because anyone so close as to be hurt by a small piece of flying plastic was going to be far more hurt by blast. More serious was the wear on the sides of the venturis. Forcing a fast-moving jet of very hot gas to turn corners is a difficult business and it produces considerable gas wash and erosion. The Burney guns partly overcame this by having jets which could be unscrewed and replaced as they wore but this was only a partial answer. The pressure in the breech rose to $1\frac{1}{2}$ tons at its peak, which is a very low figure and the muzzle-velocity was only 555ft per second so that the shell had a high trajectory and range estimation would have been critical for a successful engagement. The required range was 300yd against tanks and the Burney might just have made it, though the time of flight would have been at least $2\frac{1}{2}$ seconds which would have called for considerable judgement in order to hit a moving target.

The tour de force of the Burney shoulder gun was the shell, which was employed on most of the subsequent designs. The anti-tank shell was not hollow charge as Burney did not believe in the idea (it will be seen by now that Sir Dennis had different ideas from most people). Instead he used a shell with a thin outer wall

140

and the maximum possible amount of plastic explosive inside. On hitting a piece of armour the case split and the explosive spread out like a great lump of dough, sticking tightly to the plate. A fraction of a second later the special fuze set it off and the explosive shattered the armour rather than actually penetrating it. The intended result was to shake off a 'scab' or flake on the inside and send it ricocheting round the crew compartment at high speed, and this it usually did. At the same time the concussion was enough to incapacitate most crews without any need for missiles inside. The principle is still used and is now known as 'squash head' ammunition. There was an HE round also which went to twice the anti-tank distance and was meant to be used for engaging bunkers and machine-gun nests.

The next Burney design was a battalion anti-tank gun and again he chose an historic calibre, this time it was 3·7in, the same as the AA gun. In effect it was a scaled-up 3·45, but it had a proportionately longer barrel and a better muzzle-velocity. It was intended as a replacement for both the 6-pounder and the 17-pounder and, as it turned the scales at 377lb complete on its wheels, it looked to be an attractive proposition. Unfortunately it was a little too light and throughout its trials the carriage and trail broke in a variety of different places. Gas erosion proved to be more than had been foreseen and both the 3·45 and the 3·7 ran into continual difficulties as their trials dragged on from 1944 to 1948, when they were finally abandoned.

The two anti-tank guns were only a small part of the range of guns invented by Sir Dennis Burney, yet none of them was accepted despite the obvious merit of several of the designs. In the end one did come into service eight years after the end of the war, but only in a much modified form. It started as a 4·5in recoilless close-support gun, using the shell from the 4·5in artillery gun. It was the usual Burney principle with side jets, but the jets were placed right back on the breech block where they perhaps had less wear than if placed farther forward. The carriage was robust and there was a steel shield for the crew. Development of this gun was followed up and in 1950 it appeared as the first of the Battalion Anti-Tank Guns, or BAT series. It was finally accepted for issue in 1953, but there had been some changes over the years.

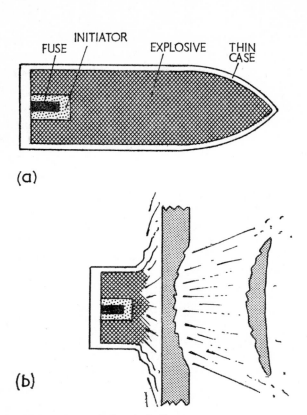

FUSE   INITIATOR   EXPLOSIVE   THIN CASE

(a)

(b)

a   High-explosive squash-head shell.
b   Squash-head shell on impact.

The BAT used a single venturi mounted on the back of the breech block in the same way as the LG 40. The base of the round had a plastic bursting disc and, instead of an offset percussion cap in the side of the case, ignition was by an electric charge conducted through a special band in the case. The carriage and wheels were massive and heavy so that the gun weighed 2,200lb which was lighter than the conventional guns of the same size but still a lot to heave around. The calibre had gone up to 120mm and although the shell alone weighed 28lb a complete unfired round was 60lb. It was both long and delicate – a knock or jar could put the shell off centre and prevent loading, or it could dent the side of the case, with the same result. It was some years before these troubles

Page 143 (*above*) Swingfire anti-tank missile at the moment of launch from a special pallet on a Land-Rover. Although the missile has only flown a short distance, it has already turned through a considerable angle, as a result of its unique jet steering system; (*below*) Milan, the Franco-German joint missile. Milan employs a semi-automatic guidance system which only requires that the operator keeps his sight on the target.

Page 144 (*above*) Robert Goddard, the American rocket pioneer, loading a solid-propellant experimental rocket into a tubular launcher in the summer of 1918. He subsequently offered this type of rocket and launcher to the US Army as a possible anti-tank weapon; (*below*) An experiment that failed. The Henschel HS 129 armed with a 50mm semi-automatic cannon. The muzzle flash and blast were too much for the pilot and the airframe, although the shell was extremely effective.

were overcome, meanwhile the rounds were kept in their transport cases which were strong steel cylinders. The weight of a complete round in one of these rose to 100lb. With so much weight the BAT and its ammunition could not possibly be towed by a jeep, and a 1-ton truck had to be used. In terms of vehicle size, crew size, ease of concealment and overall weight, the BAT was not much of an improvement over the 17-pounder, but it had one enormous advantage. It fired a deadly shell. The 120mm squash head or HESH (High Explosive Squash Head) shell caused appalling damage to a tank: tracks were blown off as if made of paper, all glass vision blocks were shattered, and all external fittings removed. Inside the effect was unspeakable and almost invariably fatal even if there were no 'scabs' flying about, but there usually were and they tended to be big.

The BAT was followed by a lighter version known as the Mobile BAT or MOBAT. One great improvement on this gun was provision for fitting a Bren light machine-gun to fire alongside the barrel. The Bren enabled the gunner to get some idea of where he was shooting without giving away the fact that he had a large-calibre gun. By firing tracers he could train his barrel on to the target and when the tracers were hitting, he could let go with the big round and have a good chance of a first-round hit. The MOBAT could be towed by a Land-Rover and although it still had an unnecessarily strong breech and a heavy barrel, it was a much better gun and is still in service with the Volunteer Reserve.

In time the MOBAT was overtaken by the WOMBAT, which was a completely new design owing little to its predecessors, except that it used the same ammunition. WOMBAT (the name is zoological and not a derivation of initials) weighs only slightly more in toto than does the barrel of MOBAT. The carriage is light and spindly, a little after the pattern of the LG 40, and only has small wheels which are for use when manhandling the gun. It is normally carried in its Land-Rover as a portee. The barrel is made from high-quality steel and as a result is very light for its size; in fact, it contributes about two-thirds of the total weight of the equipment. The breech is entirely redesigned and instead of the clumsy sliding block there is now a simple ring carrying the venturi and hinged to the barrel. It swings aside to open and locks by a bayonet joint. Traverse is by the gunner leaning against the breech, elevation by a hand wheel. It is almost as simple as the last of the German series and far more effective. The big difference lies in its aiming device which is the 0·5in spotting rifle whose projectile is matched to that of the 120mm shell so that whenever the spotting round hits, so will the shell – without fail.

There is no shield to protect the crew of WOMBAT, nor is one needed for it is more easy to camouflage and hide and with an all-up weight of only 600lb the gun can be easily moved by its crew of three. The complete round is one-tenth of the total weight of the gun, and the shell is about a twentieth; not quite a record but an admirable performance none the less. With this description of the WOMBAT, the story of British RCL guns comes to an end, and the likelihood of yet another member of the BAT family being produced does not seem possible with the advances in missile design.

The United States took up the design of recoilless guns much later than did Britain, but was able to work from a firmer foundation. Research was sparked off by a captured 10·5cm LG 40, taken in the Western Desert. After some delay a more or less exact copy was produced, chambered for the US 105mm round. At the same time the infantry took the principle for an anti-tank gun and by late 1944 the first one was undergoing trials. This was the 57mm, a 5ft-long tube weighing 40lb. The difference between this and other RCL guns of the time lay in its breech and venturis. The chamber was an enlarged cylinder with a fairly large air space around the cartridge case. At the front end it tapered into the barrel where the shell was lodged. At the rear it was closed by a circular flat plate with scalloped holes around the rim. The plate locked against the breech by a bayonet joint. The cartridge case was perforated in the same manner as the Burney guns, but differed by having a multitude of small holes rather than a few large ones. On firing, the gas first of all filled the chamber space and then forced its way out through the holes in the breech closure plate, thereby forming the reaction to the recoil. At first sight it seems as though the plate must wear out in the first few shots, but it does not and there seems to be hardly any wear from gas wash.

The first guns had a special feature all of their own, and it has not been repeated. The driving band of the shell was pre-engraved with the rifling. The idea behind this was to try to cut down the pressure needed to get the shell moving and to smooth out some of the variations in muzzle-velocity caused by uneven powder loadings and by temperature changes. In fact it did none of these things and only complicated the loader's task as he had to 'feel' for the rifling grooves while loading. As we have seen, some initial pressure is necessary to ensure that the powder burns properly, and allowing the shell to move more easily does little to help this. Anyway, whatever the part played by the pre-engraved bands, the 57mm was a success and it still is in use in some of the National Guard units in the USA and is to be found in almost every army in South-East Asia. The Chinese made their own exact copy of it and used it in Korea and it has been captured more recently in Vietnam.

The original, however, was ordered in large quantities and was one of the few recoilless guns to see service in World War II since it was taken to the Pacific and employed as a general close-support infantry gun in the closing stages of the campaign and particularly in the Philippines. Few, if any, tanks were met but the gun proved its worth and two more projects were immediately put in hand. The first was to manufacture a wide range of ammunition for the 57mm, including HE, white phosphorous smoke, and canister.

The second development was to make a larger version, this time 75mm, and this too had the complete range of ammunition. The 75mm saw a very little action in the Philippines and a good deal later on in Korea. It too has been adopted by South-East Asian countries, as well as China, who have paid the originators the unusual compliment of using their brain-child against them. The 75mm weighs a little more than the 57mm at 114lb, which is still remarkably little for the size of shell. It normally comes with a wheeled tripod and geared elevating mechanism.

In the USA, as in Britain, the active research into recoilless guns slowed down after the war to almost a dead stop, but not quite because two new ones appeared in the slack years before Korea. The first was the 90mm, a smaller and lighter gun than the 75mm but firing a shell of almost the same size. The 90 was meant for a different role, that of the defence of the infantry platoon and its range was half that of the 75 which was a company, or even battalion, gun. The 90 has survived and is still in service. Strangely it has never been adopted by the Asian countries, perhaps because Nationalist China was given none and so the communists did not capture any. At 34lb the 90 is a tidy weight to hump on one's shoulder but it is immensely sturdy and will tolerate any amount of rough handling and abuse.

In 1945 the 75mm was scaled up to 105mm and prototypes built with the intention that it should be a proper battalion gun. It remained an idea until the Korean War when it was hurriedly put together and appeared in use at the end of the war. It was never a satisfactory design for a number of reasons, one being that the trunnions were too far back and necessitated balancing springs; another that it was too heavy altogether; and another that there was no spotting rifle. An improved version at the same calibre was soon brought out and rather than call it a Mark 2 model, or some similar title, it was decided to give it another calibre altogether purely to avoid confusion – for both were exactly the same bore – so the well-known 106mm came into being. It has been phenomenally successful and must have been used at one time or another by almost every army in the Western World. It is light, weighing only 485lb, and fires an effective anti-tank shell out to 1,000yd or more with a 0·5in spotting rifle to ensure first-round hits. It is less mobile than a WOMBAT when off its jeep, but it can be broken down into two loads if need be and carried by its crew for short distances. The Austrian Army has adopted the 106mm and built their own special mount for it. This is a two-wheeled carriage with a short trail, all of robust proportions. Thus equipped, the 106mm can be towed behind a jeep at high speeds along rough roads. The idea behind this modification is to allow the gun to be towed by the wide variety of vehicles in the Austrian Army and not to confine it to one specialised jeep. So far as is known, no other country has taken such a step. In the 1950s the US Marine Corps went so far as to fit six 106s on to the turret of their then current light tank to give it increased fire-power for little increase in weight, and they named the monster Ontos. Its only use in anger was in the Dominican Republic in 1964 when it was used for blowing down houses concealing snipers.

One other country showed interest in the recoilless principle and this was Sweden. Always a leader in technical matters, the

Swedes started research into recoilless guns at about the same time as the British. As in Britain it was the brainchild of one man, an engineer named Hugo Abramson. He demonstrated a 20mm single-shot gun in 1941 and an improved version was accepted for service within two years. It was a single-venturi type, much the same as the LG 40, but to load the ammunition the complete venturi swung over to one side on a side-mounted pin and was locked back in place with a hook-shaped handle. The barrel was very long and this allowed the projectile to take full advantage of the propellant so that the muzzle-velocity was one of the highest ever for a recoilless gun, 2,950ft per second. The firing pin was central in the venturi and was operated by a long external rod. It was a good design, well engineered but too small in calibre. A 37mm was tried in 1943 but not pursued and in 1946 a start was made on what is now well known as the 84mm Carl Gustav.

Carl Gustav was adopted by the Swedish Army in 1949 and has remained in substantially the same form ever since. It has been bought by many armies all over the world, but particularly in NATO, and is one of the most successful current light anti-armour weapons. It is a short-barrelled recoilless gun with a single venturi and the same swinging breech as on the original 20mm m/42. The cartridge case has a plastic blow-out disc and the primer has to be in the side of the case. To ensure that it is in line with the firing pin, the case has to be indexed by a notch in the rim and a lug on the chamber, as was the Krupp 105 of 1943; in darkness this can be tricky to load, but with training it becomes surprisingly easy. The gun is beautifully made of high-grade steel and has a very high standard of finish on all surfaces. It is strong and reliable, but becoming somewhat outdated now and its effective range of 350yd is not adequate enough recompense for its weight of 32lb.

A still smaller recoilless gun is the cousin of Carl Gustav, the Miniman. This is a throw-away gun in the tradition of the Panzerfaust but with a greater range and accuracy. It has a wound glass-fibre barrel of 68mm containing a 2lb projectile and its propelling charge. The charge is in its own cylinder which has holes in the sides, just like a Burney shell and it acts in the same way on firing. The propellant burns, forces its way out of the

149

cylinder, builds up pressure in the breech, gives the shell its initial push, and then the entire cycle takes place with the shell going out of the muzzle and the gas going out of a crude venturi to the rear. It is all very basic: the sights are plastic and so is much of the firing gear. The projectile is unspun and steadied in flight by fins and the complete weight is 6½lb. Effective range is over 250yd, very good for so simple a weapon. It is issued in large numbers to the Swedish Army and Home Guard, though it has not had much success in foreign sales.

Another Swedish recoilless gun is the Bofors 90mm, a fairly modern battalion gun of straightforward design and performance except for the method of mounting the barrel. Instead of using trunnions and traversing pintle the Bofors hangs the barrel from an overhead ball-joint. To get the ball-joint above the barrel, it has to be carried on an odd-looking, swan-necked arm which comes up from the mount but the advantage is that the gunner has complete control of the gun by moving his shoulder and it is easy to train and aim. There is a spotting rifle and the complete gun can be either towed on its two substantial wheels or carried portee style in the Swedish jeep.

The Soviets have never shown much enthusiasm for the recoilless principle, preferring to put their trust in either rockets or conventional guns. After the war they produced an 82mm recoilless gun of undistinguished appearance with a single jet venturi through which the rounds were loaded. It was a heavy weapon and it did not stay in service in Russia for many years, although it may still be met in some of the Satellites and Jugoslavia. It was followed by a larger version of 107mm calibre which for some reason was never popular and has now disappeared altogether. Even the Satellites did not take it in quantity and it must have been a bad design to have been so completely dropped. The Czechs took the 82mm and built their own versions of it, one of which was much lighter and smaller called the Tarsnice. This had about half the range of the original model but was much handier. The other version was a streamlined model of the Soviet gun, four times as heavy, but with twice the range (to 1,000yd). The Czechs must have thought that even this was not worth the effort for it too went out of service indecently quickly.

Finland is another country which built its own design of recoilless gun, though it was never produced in any great quantity. It was known as the Model 58, from the year of its birth. It came a little late in the day since by 1958 most countries had had their guns in service for at least four years but there are signs that the Finns gained from the experience of their rivals and may well have produced one of the best of them all. The Model 58 is a 95mm gun of the remarkably low overall weight of 308lb, a substantial advance on the 572lb of the Bofors 90mm and perhaps explained in part by the fact that the Finnish gun has no spotting rifle to assist in aiming. This detracts sharply from its tactical advantage of the low weight, but even so to have produced such a light gun is an unusual achievement. It resembles the US 106mm in general outline and the breech is quite obviously a copy of the Kromuskit type used in the US series. It fires its 22lb shell at a muzzle-velocity of almost 1,800ft per second, a high figure for a recoilless gun and only exceeded by the Bofors 90mm. One would like to know more of this interesting gun, but it was obviously never made in large numbers nor was it sold to any other countries – a penalty for being late into the field. With a spotting rifle it looks as if it would have been a useful weapon.

The only other recoilless anti-tank gun which showed any originality of design was a Japanese experimental model of late 1945. It was intended as a one-man portable system and tried to combine the best features of the then current German weapons. It was a cross between a Panzershreck and an LG 43 and with luck and some sensible development might well have become a useful weapon. The calibre was 82mm which was just about adequate for the time, and the weight of the experimental model was 90lb, which again was reasonable. The breech was an almost exact copy of the LG 43 with a central firing pin and a short venturi cone. Maximum range was quoted at 850yd, but for tanks it would have been much less. There was a light tripod and an optical sight and although the general standard of engineering and finish is nowhere near that of the American 57s and 75s the principle seems to be right and perhaps the US Armour Corps can be grateful that only one was made. No ammunition survived and so no firing was done by the US Army.

8

THE MISSILE

Thing that can be thrown to do damage.
(Stones, spears & other mm. also
attrib. as m. weapons.)

The Pocket Oxford Dictionary

Now that anti-tank missiles have become a reality, it is often
wondered why it took so long for them to appear. The technology
to make them existed in World War II when the Germans had
glider bombs and wire-controlled demolition tanks. The Allies had
had radio-controlled target aircraft since before the war and
although there is a world of difference between a target aeroplane
and a tiny missile, nevertheless the principle is about the same. But
even the Germans with their astonishing span of inventions and
apparent freedom to investigate the unlikely and the unwanted,
never ventured into anti-tank missiles. It might have been a good
thing for them if they had. One must conclude that probably the
real reason for the lack of interest in missiles during the war was
because no one asked for them.

In a war the inventors and developers are very much tied by
time and the user's requirements. If the user asks for a new and
larger gun, then that is what he usually gets. For the most part the
user does not think too hard before asking: his present gun is
outranged or defeated by the armour of the tanks he is meeting, so
his reaction is to demand a bigger and better gun – quickly. Faced
with this demand and a tight timetable, the developers give him
what he asked for – a bigger gun. When the user screams that it is
too heavy, he has only himself to blame, and much development
time is lost in trying to refine the result. If the user had asked in the
first place for a better way of defeating tanks, the weapon he gets

might be quite different from a gun and it is this argument that is applied to the theory that anti-tank guided missiles could possibly have been made and used in World War II. Since no one did so ask, the armoury was restricted to guns alone, with a few light rockets, and nothing else; the missiles had to fight their way through post-war financial restrictions and military indifference.

The first missiles appeared in the mid-1950s and were French. Before examining the features of these various devices, it will be as well to briefly revise the jargon which is used in their description and also to run over the ways in which they are fired and guided.

Strictly speaking all objects which are projected or fired are missiles, whether they be the smooth round stones slung by David against Goliath, or the multi-ton monster rockets carrying nuclear warheads half-way around the world. Common usage has narrowed the word down to mean more or less those objects which are propelled by rocket motors and which fly at the commands of those who launched them, and which carry some sort of explosive warhead. We shall use this definition. Guided missiles are those which are expressly under the control of the launch personnel throughout the flight and here the definitions and meanings become a little woolly since most rocket missiles fall into this category, but again common use (or misuse) has brought this term to mean those which are guided for their entire flight and this specifically refers to those which are fired against tanks since they are under control from beginning to end.

The great majority of anti-tank missiles are wire-guided. This means that the missile is controlled by electrical signals sent to it in flight along a pair of fine wires which trail behind it. The commands are simple in the extreme and are confined to movement in the two planes, up and down, and left and right. Nothing more is needed except that on certain practice missiles it is usually necessary to programme the missile to destroy itself if it flies grossly off course or goes beyond the range boundary. This is done by including one extra command signal. The wire is remarkably fine and is insulated to prevent shorting during flight. It is carried in the tail of the missile and unwound in flight by being pulled off its spool or bobbin as the missile flies along. It is usually so thin that it scarcely has time to float to the ground before the missile has completed its flight. The wire has to be carried in the missile as this is the only way in which it will not be put under strain. It would be impossible to expect a rocket to pull the wire from a stationary bobbin at the launch site, but the method used has the disadvantage that the missile has to carry the weight of the whole length of wire and has to pay it out evenly and rapidly during the flight. The apparently simple matter of paying out wire has built up an entire new technical art which is by no means at the end of study yet. Apart from the unwinding problems, there is the fact that, as the wire is unwound, the weight of missile changes which may give trouble in flight and control, so that the mechanical difficulties in themselves are large enough without adding electrical and electronic ones on top.

When compared to a gun, a missile offers tremendous advantages. It needs only a very simple launcher, and often no launcher at all, and it can carry a very large warhead. Because it is guided, there is a very high probability of a hit, much more so than with a gun. The great point about missile accuracy is that, provided the operator can see the target, he can hit it just as easily at maximum range as at any other range. In fact a target close to the launcher is usually the most difficult of all to hit because the time of flight is too short to get the missile under control. This is the complete opposite of the gun situation where the closer the range, the better. The medium-sized missiles can already outrange the conventional guns and all indications are that this will continue and the guns will not be able to catch up. By having a simple launcher a missile is very easily moved and even more easily concealed. There is no muzzle flash and no blast and the great majority of modern missiles are all but invisible from start to finish of their flight. The tank has no idea that it is being fired at, and no way of locating the launcher when it does find out. With an anti-tank gun there is always the chance that the muzzle blast will be spotted, and by weaving about the driver can put the gunner off his aim to a certain extent. With a missile he can weave and twist as much as he likes for it makes no difference, the missile controller can follow every manoeuvre with no trouble at all.

But the missile does have its drawbacks, for nothing is quite perfect, and this is particularly so with the older types which use

154

manual guidance. In order to give the gunner (or operator) a chance to guide the flight, the missile usually flies quite slowly, say 300–400mph. To cover 2,000yd at 400mph takes ten seconds; at 300mph, it is thirteen seconds. A lot can happen in thirteen seconds. For instance the target can go behind a tree or house, or it can just move behind some thin cover that the operator cannot see through. He becomes helpless since, if he cannot see the target, he cannot hit it.

Since missiles fly at aeroplane speeds, it is usual to control them by aeroplane methods and most of the early models used elevators and ailerons which operated in the airstream. This system has the advantage that it is simple and cheap to build and by fitting in a gyroscope the commands can be sent to the appropriate control surface to execute whatever manoeuvre is required. A gyro is necessary since it cannot be guaranteed that the missile will remain in the attitude in which it took off, and in some missiles it is purposely arranged that it shall slowly roll over and over during flight to cancel out any irregularities in the manufacture or in the line of thrust. The elevators are attached to small wings or fins – all these slow-flying missiles need some sort of wing to keep them up and to keep them flying more or less straight.

But there is a drawback to simple aerodynamic control surfaces: they require wind to make them work, which means that until the missile gets up to its proper flying speed, it is not under full control, and in the critical period just after launch, it is hardly under control at all. This usually means that the minimum range is quite long, or in other words it has to travel a long way before it can be guided to a target and so tanks are immune to all but a lucky hit if they can get close enough – a curious reversal of the gun principle where the shorter the range the more accurate the shooting. To overcome this the more modern missiles fit the control surfaces actually in the jet stream from the nozzle. Naturally this means that the vanes have to be of some special heat-resisting material but in compensation they can take effect from the instant that the motor starts. This is the control method used in the British Swingfire and we will later deal with other features of this weapon. The jet-control arrangement enables Swingfire to make astounding manoeuvres within a very few feet of leaving the launch box.

Most, but not all, missiles are controlled by a man with a control box and a small joystick or some variation of one. This joystick heightens the likeness to an aeroplane and a few missiles, particularly the Soviet ones, have a control box whose features are very similar indeed to those of a radio-controlled model aeroplane. The operator controls his missile by looking through a telescope or a pair of binoculars and guides his missile along his line of sight by moving the joystick in exactly the same way as does a pilot. He can see his missile by the bright blaze of the rocket motor and in some models this is further enhanced by adding a special flare in the tail. The commands sent along the wires move the control surfaces and the operator judges how much to move them and when to back them off. It is a task which requires a certain amount of skill and plenty of practice, but the difficulty of it is very largely determined by the type of control system employed. There are two, and it is important in the study of any modern missiles to be able to understand what is involved in each.

Nearly all the early missiles used what is now known as 'acceleration control'. In this arrangement when the joystick is put over to one side, say the left, the missile turns left. When the stick is centralised – no more turn is needed – the missile straightens out, but only straightens out on its new course, so it is still travelling to the left at an angle to its original flight line. It is exactly what happens in a motor car: if the steering wheel is turned to the left for a few seconds and then straightened, the car travels off to the left in a straight line. If the steering wheel is kept on a left lock, the car will continue to turn left and ultimately cover a complete circle. A missile will do the same: if the stick is not centralised, it will continue to turn in a circle, the size of the circle depending on how much the stick is moved. To try to explain what this means to the controller, let us imagine that he needs to shift his missile to the left to bring it on to the line of sight. He puts on left stick and takes it off again as the missile moves across. At some point just before the missile meets the line of sight, he must put on right stick to straighten it up, and what usually happens is that he either over- or undercorrects and another command has to be put on, and another, and so on, so that the flight is a constant movement of the missile up, down and to either side of the line of sight.

The 'velocity control' system is slightly different and relies on a more complex gyro for its success. In this system, when the stick is moved to the left, the missile turns left; but when the stick is centralised, the missile turns back an equal amount to the right – and ends up travelling on a parallel path to its original flight. It cuts out the guesswork in the correction of the movement and places much less strain on the controller. In effect, what it does is to displace the missile in the direction of the stick movement rather than an actual turn. The advantage of this arrangement is that when a demand is given to the missile it always appears to the operator to move at a constant speed across his line of sight; with acceleration control the missile appears to move faster and faster, hence the term 'acceleration control', and it can be difficult to bring the missile back on to the intended course. With velocity control the operator can 'nudge' the missile across and on to a target by giving it little jabs on the control stick, but this is quite impossible with an acceleration-control missile. Of the two, acceleration control requires much more training and refresher training.

Despite the drawbacks to acceleration control, it has been used on several missiles because it is easier to make and easier to maintain; though in truth there is little maintenance required on a modern missile – it either works or it does not, and if it does not, it is returned to the maker. The first practical anti-tank missiles were built in the mid-1950s by the French firm of Nord Aviation using as their inspiration a World War II German air-to-air missile called Ruhrstahl which was still in the development stage at the end of the war. The first model was the SS 10 which stayed in service for six years or more before being replaced by the SS 11, a larger version. SS 10 was reasonably big for its time; it weighed 33lb, was just under 3ft long, and had a wing span of 30in. There were four wings or fins and they sloped back at a steep angle. It flew at an average speed of 80m per second, or roughly 180mph, and the range was 1,600m. SS 10 was too slow and had too short a range, but it was the first anti-tank missile ever to be put into service and it was successful. It therefore has its place in history. There are reports, unconfirmed for the most part, that it was used by the French Army in Algeria for taking out point targets in difficult country; such items as hill-top strong points and cave

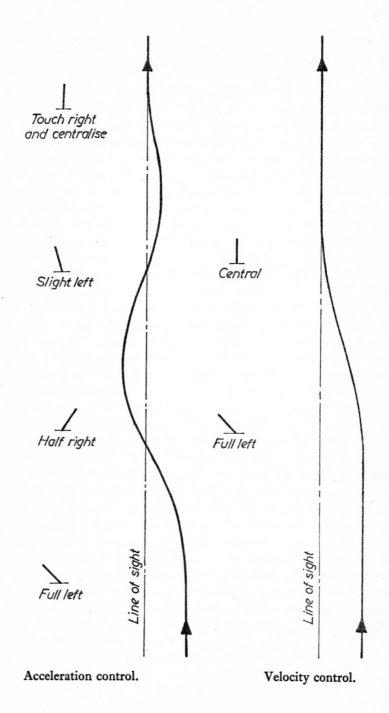

Touch right
and centralise

Slight left

Central

Half right

Full left

Full left

Line of sight

Line of sight

Acceleration control.

Velocity control.

defences have been mentioned as being destroyed by its hollow-charge warhead when it was difficult or impossible to bring up conventional artillery.

The greatest contribution made by SS 10 was that it showed that it could be done, and it introduced some useful ideas at the same time. The launch apparatus was the box in which the missile travelled, an idea that has been copied by many since. The lid was removed, the front end propped up, the sight plugged into the back and the missile was ready for firing. It was the truly one-man tank killer. But it was not good enough nor was it powerful enough and it was replaced in the late 1950s by SS 11. SS 11 was twice the weight and had a much bigger warhead; it was 46in long but less in wing span – 20in. The cruising speed was nearly doubled to 335mph and the maximum range increased to 3,000m. It was a formidable weapon and a successful one, for it was bought and put into service by more than twenty countries. The all-up weight of 30 kilograms (66lb) includes a warhead which will penetrate more than 23in of armour plate – a startling performance and a good example of the ability of missiles to carry large quantities of explosive. To put a similar amount of explosive into a shell, it would have to be of the order of 155mm calibre and its gun would weigh 5 or 6 tons. SS 11 is used not only from its box launcher, but is also mounted and fired from vehicles. It can be carried on a jeep in its boxes, arranged so that they fire from outriggers on either side, or in some cases over the top of the windscreen. With this type of mounting the driver and operator dismount and go some yards to one side to avoid the launch blast. On armoured cars and tanks, the missiles are either in boxes or on rails at the sides of the turret. There is hardly any limit to the ways in which it can be put on to vehicles and, in a very slightly modified version, it is carried on side rails on helicopters.

SS 11 has been the backbone of the anti-tank defence of the French Army for more than ten years, but its weight was rather too high for an infantry man-portable missile and shortly after its introduction a variant was built, known as Entac, an acronym from Engin Teleguide Anti Chars (anti-tank guided missile). It is smaller and lighter than SS 11, 70lb in its box, 26lb in flight, with a maximum range of 2,000m. The warhead is light, containing only 8lb of explosive, but this is sufficient for an impressive penetration of more than 20in of armour, although the hole may be quite small. Entac was adopted by the French Army in 1957 and has been bought by Australia, Belgium, Canada, Indonesia, and the USA, either for trials or for service use. By 1968 128,000 had been ordered and 116,000 delivered. This makes it look as if it has been a money spinner for the firm in the same class as SS 11.

Continuing the French story, the next missile was SS 12, but this was definitely a vehicle-mounted missile and as such is moving towards the same idea as the self-propelled gun which we agreed not to discuss in this book. Sufficient to say therefore that it is a larger version of the SS 11, with a corresponding change in the propulsion system. It has semi-automatic guidance and was probably the first missile to go into service with such a system. It is worth digressing at this point to explain semi-automatic guidance and its principles of operating. The basic idea is the same in all systems: when the missile is fired, all that the operator has to do is to keep his sight laid correctly on the target, no matter how it moves. The missile then flies down his line of sight regardless of how that line is shifted about. This is done by building a complicated guidance box which contains infra-red sensors. These sensors detect the presence of the missile flare in the field of view of the sight, and they emit electrical signals to a suitable translational unit which then sends correcting signals down the wires to the missile telling it which way to move to come into the centre. When it is in the centre, all messages stop and it is left to fly on; however, it rarely stays still and there are continuous corrections. The missile itself requires hardly any changes to incorporate semi-automatic guidance, but it can be seen from this simple explanation that the sight unit requires to be formidably complicated and delicate, and this inevitably leads to greatly increased cost. The advantages of semi-automatic guidance are almost overwhelming when laid against the straightforward criterion of hitting the target, for all the operator has to do is to press his trigger and keep his sights on the target and he cannot miss. Furthermore, the training of a man to do this is very simple. But nothing is really straightforward in weaponry.

Not only is the cost high, but semi-automatic guidance brings with it a tactical penalty also. The operator must be in a place where he can clearly see and where he can have his missile right alongside him so that as it is launched, it flies off down the line of sight. As he swings his sight from side to side, the missile must swing with it. This calls for a firing position that is to some extent exposed to enemy view though one hopes that it is far enough back from the enemy positions for it to be very difficult to spot. With the manual guidance by joystick, the operator does not need to be near his missile when he launches it. He can take his control box to another place and, provided it is connected by wire to the missile-launcher, he can fire and control it from several yards away from the launch point. The actual distance that this can be done is usually carefully classified and not printed for general consumption, but it has been suggested that 50–100m is not impossible to achieve. On firing, the operator has to bring his missile over to his line of sight and then fly it to the target as normally. This initial swing requires a good deal of training, and also uses up the first few hundred yards of flight, but it means that the operator can be hidden on a hill-top and his missiles can be just behind the hill so that the actual launch is completely concealed. This is an enormous advantage as a missile is most likely to be seen at launch; in flight it is to all intents and purposes invisible. With proper siting and good controllers, it is possible to knock out tanks without their having the slightest idea where the missiles are coming from or who is operating them. There are some indications that this may have happened at times in the 1973 Arab-Israeli War. The greatest disadvantage to the separated controller is the amount of minimum range used up in getting the missile on to the sight line. This explains why many missiles are listed as having an effective range of from 300–400m out to their maximum, the 300–400m being needed to get the missile under control. The semi-automatic guidance system does not suffer from this, as the missile goes off down the line sight just like a shell from a gun.

Returning to the French missile family, the next and last one is Milan, a man-portable, semi-automatically guided missile of advanced design. It has just come into service in the French Army and will shortly be in service with the German Army, after ten years of development and trials. Milan introduces several new concepts. The first is the prepackaged missile. The missile is delivered from the factory, and carried into action in a glass-fibre tube which is actually loaded into the back of the launcher barrel so that it forms part of the breech, if not the actual breech itself. On firing the carrying tube is ejected to the rear and the launcher is ready for a fresh round. It is simple to operate and extremely effective. The missile is 30in long and in its tube weighs 24lb. The launch unit is another 33lb, so that the total weight of a loaded launcher is more than an infantry soldier is going to carry unaided for any great distance, but the loading sequence is so easy and fast that any movement would normally be done with the round unloaded. There are no checks to be done before firing, the entire equipment is considered as a gun and its ammunition and, if a round misfires, it is rejected and another loaded. It flies at 590ft per second, or just over 400mph – which is fast. One advantage of this higher speed is that the missile can be fired in an emergency at close range as an ordinary direct-fire shell, without using the guidance at all, and the claimed minimum range is 75m when used in this way. Milan can be seen to be a most useful weapon, and a far cry from the earlier rather fragile, slow-moving missiles of the 1950s. However, like any other semi-automatic guided missile, it is expensive.

Although the French were first in the field of guided anti-tank missiles, it was not long before other countries produced their own and by 1960 there was almost a miniature flood of them, all joystick controlled and most of them quite small. In Germany Messerschmitt produced the Cobra, which first went into service in 1960 and was said to be still in production in 1969. It was a 23lb missile of conventional design with four wings, a warhead weighing 5lb, and a claimed range of 2,000m. Its only peculiarity was that it needed no launcher box nor rail. It was fired from off the ground, resting on two of its wings. There was an external booster rocket on the outside of the body, and on firing this caused the Cobra to jump upwards and forwards. After a few yards, the main motor lit up and the missile flew normally and could be gathered by the controller. It was reasonably priced and appeared attractive to those countries with no missile industry of their own. By 1969 over 120,000 had been made and sold to eighteen countries, among them many of NATO. It is a slow flier, 190mph, and its big wings are probably unduly affected by cross winds.

In Italy the Mosquito is much the same as the Cobra, except that it is launched from its carrying box. It is very slightly bigger than Cobra, but has a warhead of roughly the same size and flight characteristics which closely approximate. It is said to be still in production, but it has not been sold in any great number to other countries. Sweden has the Bantam, an acronym for Bofors Anti-Tank Missile. This started as a private venture of the Bofors company in 1956 and was adopted by the Swedish Army in 1963 and the Swiss Army in 1967. Although it claims to have nearly the same dimensions as Cobra, that is a length of 3ft and a span of 16in, the weight is less – only 17lb – so that one must expect the warhead to be correspondingly smaller and less effective. The wings telescope into their mountings in order to reduce the size of the carrying box and they pop out on launch. Bantam is fired from its box like SS 11 and in the Swiss Army is carried on a special mounting on the front of the military Puch-Haflinger mini-jeeps.

Even Japan has a first generation missile, the KAM-3. It was designed in 1957 and has been in service since 1963. It, again, resembles the Cobra, but is bigger. It is launched from a light cradle placed on the ground and it is claimed to be a simple missile to control. One photograph which appears in an international weapons book purports to show it being fired at night and, if this is true, the KAM-3 is one of the very few which have been so fired, for a missile is very nearly impossible to use at night because the flare and motor glare obliterate the target when the missile is aimed correctly and the gunner cannot see with any precision where the target is and so cannot make the fine adjustments which make the difference between a hit and a miss. There is now a second-generation KAM-3 with semi-automatic guidance, but this is a vehicle-mounted missile and so outside the scope of pure infantry-carried or operated missiles.

In Britain there was as much interest in missiles as in other countries and in 1956 Messrs Vickers started their own private-venture studies for an ATGW. The result was Vigilant which went into service in 1963 and was promptly sold to Finland and Kuwait. In 1964 it was bought in quantity by Saudi Arabia and in

163

the next year by Libya. Vigilant is very similar to all the other missiles in general outline and performance although possessing smaller wings because of a higher flying speed. It is launched from its carrying box, into which it is packed at the factory, and guided by a thumbstick rather than an actual joystick. The range is short, 1,370m, but the accuracy is good. Vigilant is the only one of the first-generation missiles not to use acceleration control. Vickers pioneered the velocity-control system and accepted that it would be more expensive. It has been proved to be worth the extra cost and the accuracy record of Vigilant is impressively high. It is a true one-man weapon with a light control box and sight. The missile is steered by aerodynamic control surfaces so that it has to get to speed before responding properly to demands, but the minimum range is less than with any of the other first-generation models and its reliability and ruggedness are very good. It is its misfortune that it came a little late into the field and found that most of the market was already filled with other models of poorer perform-ance.

The second British missile is Swingfire, a larger version of the Vigilant and far more powerful and versatile. Swingfire is of a unique design which does not appear on any other anti-tank mis-sile. From the exterior it appears to be another wire-guided, man-controlled, first-generation GW, but it is actually much more than that. It is large and fast but the guidance is different from any others that have been made. The operator controls it by a thumb-stick very like the Vigilant and the missile is velocity controlled, but by rotating and deflecting the motor jet. This is a very sig-nificant improvement since it means that the missile is under complete control from the moment that the motor is fired and so the minimum range of Swingfire is extremely short. Another feature of Swingfire is the computing sight and programmed flight package. The controller can be placed a considerable distance from the missile in any direction and on firing the missile will fly on a programmed course which will bring it into the line of sight and flying towards the target so that the operator can pick it up and gather it. This automatic flight programming can be computed for large arcs of fire and the operator can be quite confident that, wherever he points his sight within the specified arc when he fires the missile, it will turn immediately and bring itself into his field of view without any action on his part. This is most valuable as it reduces the training required for a controller and makes it possible for him to take up tactical positions which would not be possible with the older types of missile. Swingfire is in service with the British Army and is fully operational.

The United States stayed clear of the initial rush to build first-generation missiles and contented herself with buying a few SS 11 and Entac to gain experience and knowledge. The US Army was not convinced that it could get full value from the joystick-guided models, and after a brief flirtation with a vehicle-mounted design called Dart, it was decided to start a full-blown study to produce a semi-automatically guided missile without going through the joystick stage at all. This was to prove neither easy nor cheap nor quick. Studies started in 1960, and the first missile was not operational until 1972; however, it was worth waiting for. It is called TOW, an acronym for Tube-launched, Optical-tracked, Wire-guided missile. It is large, much larger than Milan, heavy, expensive, and complicated, but enormously powerful and very effective. It can be mounted on a helicopter without requiring any changes to the missile, though the sighting system has to be entirely different, and in the closing stages of the Vietnam war, two TOW-carrying helicopters had an 80 per cent success rate against Viet-Cong tanks and armoured vehicles. The missiles were fired while the helicopters were flying straight and level towards the target, using a special stabilised sight.

On its ground mount, TOW weighs 170lb, a serious load for its crew of four men. The missile itself weighs almost 40lb in its launch tube and like Milan this tube remains behind when the missile is launched. A small recoilless charge blows the missile out on its course and the rocket motor lights up when it is under way. The back-blast from the launch charge is enough to disturb camouflage which could be embarrassing in dusty conditions, and because the launcher has to be in view of the target it follows that the target can see it and thus the launch signature. However, this is a small price to pay for such an efficient weapon and the US Army is in no doubt that it has the best possible anti-tank weapon in use today. The range is quoted as being well over a mile with pin-point accuracy all the way and a short time of flight so that the chances of the target moving behind cover are much less than with many of the older designs, and the strain on the gunner is reduced also as he is not expected to track his tank for more than a few seconds.

The second US design is Dragon, a truly man-portable missile. As with TOW, it is semi-automatically guided and it uses the usual systems for tracking and passing the commands to the missile. It is 90mm in diameter and the missile is delivered in a fibre-glass tube which forms the complete launch apparatus. The gunner simply attaches his sight/tracker unit to the tube to make up the complete Dragon system. He carries his sight with him, but empty missile tubes are discarded. However, Dragon is not a miniature TOW, it is quite different. The propulsion system is unique in missiles and to the layman it seems incredible that it works at all. There is no single large rocket motor in the tail as all the others have; instead, there are sixty tiny motors arranged in twelve lines down the central portion of the body, each inclined at an angle so that the motors fire backwards and outwards. These motors fire only for a short time, less than a second, and they are initiated in pairs from both ends of the line at the same time so that there is no pitching up or down motion.

When the gunner anticipates a target, he attaches the tracker to a tube, extends the light bipod legs, and sets up a firing position. When he has a target in the sights, he presses the trigger and the Dragon is launched by the usual small recoilless charge and it rolls slowly as it flies. After a few yards of free flight, the first pair of rockets is fired. A gyro determines when the selected rockets are facing downwards and they are fired towards the ground. The effect is to give the Dragon a thrust upward and forward and successive pairs of rockets are fired at roughly half-second intervals throughout the flight to overcome the effects of gravity and wind drag. As each pair fires, the missile rises slightly in its flight and as it loses velocity curves gently down again, whereupon another pair fires below it and the process continues until it reaches the target. The noise of a Dragon is quite distinctive and at night the bursts of flame from the rockets make twinkling points of light as the almost-dark missile shoots down the range, whilst a time exposure on a camera shows the flight to resemble a string of bright beads on a long line of light. By day, watching a Dragon firing, one is irresistibly reminded of a small dog bounding through the long grass.

The semi-automatic guidance in the sight feeds the necessary corrections and when a side movement is required, the gyro waits until the missile is canted at an angle before firing the next pair so that the offset thrust pushes it back on course. After firing, the gunner disconnects his tracker unit from the empty launch tube, discards the tube, and is ready for another shot. The total weight of the Dragon, as set up to shoot, is 30lb and the tracker unit is less than 7lb of that total. The missile has a large hollow-charge warhead whose performance is obviously heavily classified, but the manufacturer has released sufficient information to show that it penetrates the armour of all present-day tanks, no matter at what angle it strikes. The only apparent drawback to Dragon seems to be its range. This is in the vicinity of one kilometre, or 1,100yd, which is not excessive by any means. Vigilant was criticised in its original version for having too little range when it offered 1,375m and the later models went out to 1,700m, so Dragon may be behind in this area. It seems doubtful if it could be extended with the present propulsion system, although it would be most unwise to underestimate the resourcefulness and ingenuity of its manufacturers.

The final country to be considered in the field of anti-tank missiles is Soviet Russia and it is a frustrating subject to address since the flow of information from Russia is so meagre and so slanted by propaganda that it is difficult to arrive at any firm conclusions. We do know, however, that there are at least three ATGW in the Soviet armoury and by now there may be more. However, of the ones we know, the oldest is the PUR-61, known to NATO as Snapper. Snapper is very like the SS 11 and is roughly the same size and weight. As far as can be judged, it has a range bracket of 500–2,300m and probably flies quite slowly since the wings are large and cruciform in their way of mounting. It is aerodynamically steered and has a hollow-charge warhead. It would be fair to give it all the characteristics of SS 11 and equally fair to assume that it is an acceleration-control type of guidance system. Although an infantry weapon, Snapper is usually mounted on multiple launchers or vehicles. There is a provision for the operator to be separated by a distance of up to 50m.

Shortly after the introduction of Snapper it was supplemented by another missile, called the PUR-62 in the Soviet Army, but known to NATO as Swatter. Swatter is more of a mystery and less is known about it despite the time that it has been in service (since the mid-1960s) but it seems to be an improved Snapper and it is possible that it has some sort of terminal guidance in the nose. This would mean that in the last few hundred metres of flight some sensing arrangement would detect the tank target and guide the missile straight on to it. If so, it is well ahead of its time and most sophisticated since it is managing to do all these complicated things within a very small space and it has been in service for several years already. It may be many more years before we know the real truth. The wings on Swatter are much smaller than on Snapper and it obviously flies considerably faster. It is normally vehicle borne and there has been no suggestion so far that it can be dismounted in a purely infantry role.

The third and last Soviet missile is the PUR-64 Sagger. It was first seen in 1965 and although more compact than the other two, it is thought to have the same warhead and effectiveness. It has a slightly longer body than its stablemates and quite small wings mounted at the extreme rear. From the look of these wings in one somewhat blurred photograph, it appears that they have no control surfaces and this could only mean that control is achieved by swivelling the jet as on Swingfire. If this is so, the Soviets have kept remarkably quiet about it – which is not their custom when they think they have scored a first with an invention – but it is difficult to see how else Sagger is guided. It can be launched from the ground for there is a clear photograph in existence showing it being prepared for firing on a simple cradle placed in the snow, but apart from these facts it remains a vague figure in the missile world. There is no information to be had on the sight system nor the guidance. If Swatter really does have some sort of terminal guidance, it could be that Sagger is semi-automatically guided, but we do not know and one may be sure that the Kremlin is not telling.

In the 1973 Arab-Israeli War the Sagger was fired off in great quantities by the Arab armies and seems to have been remarkably effective. However, to some extent the Arabs went against all the accepted Western ideas of using missiles for they frequently fired them in volleys of three or four. They obviously had plenty available and to make doubly sure of a hit they used this incredibly expensive 'scatter-gun' method. Even so, they often missed and there are several reports of Israeli tanks driving about the battlefield draped with long skeins of control wires dropped on to them by Saggers.

Presumably the volley-firing method was used to overcome some deficiencies in the ability of the operator. It must have almost caused heart failure to the Russian 'advisors' to see such waste, and it is certainly not a Soviet policy – so far as we know – to use missiles in that way. However, when the Saggers did hit, they put the tank right out of action and there is not the slightest doubt that they are very deadly indeed.

9
AND SOME FELL BY
THE WAYSIDE...

Necessity is the Mother of Invention.

Anon

The development of any weapon system entails a certain amount of hit-and-miss philosophy, the degree of each depending on the enthusiasm of the inventor and the gullibility of many different interests involved in the design. Some of the unsuccessful systems were so extraordinary that one wonders how any normal engineer could have been associated with them. Others are just developments of existing systems which for one good reason or another could never find space on the production line. The first idea comes into this latter category.

The success of the Mauser anti-tank rifle in 1918 heartened the German High Command and it was decided to try a machine-gun version. One was made, again by Mauser, using the Maxim action. In fact the gun was little more than a scaled-up Maxim, just as the rifle had been a scaled-up Mauser. It apparently worked, but the war ended before more than one had been finished, and that was finally put into a museum in Berlin. There it remained until it was completely destroyed in an Allied air raid in 1944. A few photographs remain. So ended a weapon that could have been a great trouble to the Allied tank force had it been pursued a little earlier in the war. A machine-gun that could actually knock out tanks would have been invaluable to the German Army; not only would it have been cheaper than the field guns they were forced to use, it would also have released those guns for proper artillery tasks, and there is every reason to believe that a 13mm machine-gun would have stopped the early tanks with the first burst.

At the same time, the summer of 1918, a proposal was put forward to the American Army for a light one-man, anti-tank rocket-launcher. The protagonist was Dr R. H. Goddard who became one of America's leading rocket pioneers. He designed a variety of rocket-launchers and recoilless guns, finally selecting a 2in-calibre rocket as the most suitable for an infantry anti-tank weapon. The launch tube was 66in long, weighed 7½lb, and was supported at the front on the firer's shoulder and at the rear by a light bipod. This arrangement was intended to allow the best possible free traverse for engaging moving targets. The rocket was 20in long, weighed 8½lb and this weight included a 4lb warhead. Some tests and demonstrations were carried out at Aberdeen Proving Ground in early November 1918, and a maximum range of 750yd was obtained, which was encouraging. The Armistice stopped any further development of Dr Goddard's work, which was most fortunate for tanks and tank crews in the first three years of World War II. Had the European armies carried bazookas in 1939, instead of anti-tank rifles, the history of the blitzkrieg might have been very different.

In the inter-war years the two innovations which caused most change in weaponry were the Gerlich squeeze-bore guns and the hollow charge. Gerlich had only a transitory influence but there were some interesting developments in his theory. One concerned the Polish Marosczek anti-tank rifle. It was realised in 1938 that the original rifle was becoming outdated and a team went to work to improve it by changing it to a squeeze bore. They had just completed their final drawings when the Germans invaded and the team had to flee to France. Here they continued and by the spring of 1940 the first two prototypes were ready for firing – whereupon the Germans invaded again and this time there was no taking the drawings or models to another country. The rifle was lost and has never reappeared.

In Germany the terrible difficulties of the Russian campaign, particularly the success of the T-34, caused a spate of inventions and trials, most of them unco-ordinated. One of the most successful anti-tank guns had been the 50cm PAK 38, but it was ham-

171

pered by a lack of mobility, just as is any other towed gun. Since the 37mm PAK 36 had been so successful on the Junkers 87, it seemed natural to try the PAK 38 in a plane, and both Mauser and Rheinmetall were given contracts to produce an automatic 5cm gun. A similar requirement (for an automatic large-calibre gun) came at the same time from the Luftwaffe who were finding it increasingly difficult to deal with the heavily defended formations of American day bombers. The Rheinmetall gun was chosen and fitted into four or five different aircraft, among them the Junkers 88, Messerschmitt 410 and the Henschel Hs 129. The gun came in a special pack which slung below the fuselage and the long barrel stuck well out in front of the nose. The operation was by recoil and the ammunition was fed from a belt whose container was wrapped around the breech mechanism. It was a compact design, but the entire pack weighed more than 1,200lb, which effectively ruined any aerobatic performance in air-to-air fighting. It was also a drawback for ground-strafing, though not so drastic a one. There were, however, other troubles. The recoil was considerable and the muzzle flash nearly blinded the pilot even with an elaborate 'pepper-pot' muzzle brake. Although immensely ingenious, the airborne PAK 38 was not a great success. An attempt to fit the 75mm PAK 40 into aeroplanes was even less worthwhile. The gun was too heavy, the rate of fire too low, and the muzzle blast and recoil too much for either pilot or airframe. About twenty Henschel 129s were fitted with the 75, and a few were put into the ill-fated Heinkel 177. As before, Rheinmetall did the conversion to semi-automatic firing, using an ingenious loading system and pneumatic rammer that permitted the original PAK 40 breech to be used without modification.

The weight and recoil of these conventional guns spurred the German High Command to push for aircraft recoilless weapons of large calibre. The main reason for this need was the relative ineffectiveness of normal armaments against the long-range day bomber, but there was at the same time a secondary anti-tank use which was stressed in the specification. Rheinmetall were still working on their answer to that requirement when the war ended, but by then they had a fairly clear idea of what they might have made. It was a 5·5cm automatic recoilless gun – the first the world would have seen. When work was stopped, development was well advanced and there is no reason to believe that the final version would not have been perfectly successful. The rounds were fed into the breech by a belt and a reciprocating breech block in exactly the same way as with any other machine-gun. The cartridge case looked exactly like the conventional type, but it differed in being made of thick paper with a combustible nitrated base. A short brass stub held the central primer and the round was fired in the normal way, the base providing obturation at the breech. As the propellant burned so did the case, thereby allowing the powder gases to come into contact with the chamber walls. A single tube leading off from the chamber led the gases by a long path around the top of the automatic loading mechanism to a venturi placed at the extreme rear of the gun, where they vented to atmosphere and balanced the recoil of the projectile. A small gas port in the chamber led some more gas to a piston which operated the breech block in the conventional way, extracting the cartridge case and feeding another round. It was a remarkable combination of the conventional and the unconventional and the Rheinmetall engineers had reached the point at which they were firing single shots from a prototype to discover the precise venturi shape to achieve recoillessness. There was some difficulty with the ammunition, which remained unsolved, in that the heavy 5·5cm shells tended to come out of the paper cases. The planned rate of fire was 300 rounds per minute at a muzzle-velocity of 2,000ft per second, which would have made it a difficult weapon for any tank to withstand.

Another Rheinmetall recoilless aircraft gun which never saw the light of day was the G 104, to be of 365mm calibre, or 14·3in! This of course was pure fantasy for there were enough rockets which could carry a warhead of that size without needing to go to a recoilless gun with the great weight of barrel involved in it; but that is exactly what the Rheinmetall engineers proposed to do. They built one and mounted it on a railway flat car to test the blast effects and to prove the recoillessness of their brainchild. This barrel was 10m long (32ft) and had a muzzle brake at each end. It fired an armour-piercing shell weighing 1,400lb at 1,000ft per second and balanced that by projecting the very heavy cartridge case as a counter-weight. One is surprised at the enormous weight of the shell, but the few surviving German documents confirm 1,400lb as the planned figure. The barrel was to be carried slung beneath the fuselage of a Junkers 88, which machine one might think would be hard-pressed to stagger off the ground with such a load, and it was to be fired in a 60–80° dive. A Junkers was actually fitted with a barrel, but it never flew. The whole monstrous idea was dropped, but one marvels that it got as far as it did – there cannot have been any pilots in the design team.

Another Rheinmetall project (they were an inventive firm) was the SG 113 7·7cm anti-armour recoilless gun. This was also novel in that it fired vertically downwards through the fuselage of the plane carrying it, shooting a 45mm discarding-sabot solid shot downwards at a velocity of 2,100ft per second and a counter-weight upwards. The firing circuit was to be triggered by a magnetic detector or a radar set which was activated by tank-sized metal objects directly underneath the plane. A similar idea, with a cluster of barrels pointing skywards, had been tried in attacks on bombers, with the fighter flying beneath the formation where it was comparatively safe from defensive machine-gun fire. Tanks, however, are much smaller targets than bombers and the SG 113 might have needed a most sophisticated electronic computer to decide just when to let its projectiles go. As it happens, the idea never got as far as a practical trial, but for sheer way-out optimism it takes a lot of beating.

A much more mundane project, which can be attributed to Germany though it was actually made and tried in the Skoda works in Czechoslovakia, was an automatic 5cm anti-tank gun for ground use. At least one was built and tried and it survives today. A clip of six rounds was fed into a hopper above the breech and the gun fired them off, using recoil as the operating force. Weight reduction was the paramount consideration and as a result strength and reliability suffered to the extent that the whole idea was abandoned after much work and thought had been put into it. Even if it had worked, it would have been most expensive to make, though it would undoubtedly have been effective. The same reasoning swayed the British who dabbled with automatic 2-pounders and 6-pounders from 1941–3, but the only result was a naval version of the 6-pounder which went into motor gunboats.

Aircraft mountings for anti-tank weapons consumed a good deal of design time and effort throughout the war. The simplest arrangements were the straightforward fitting of a ground gun into the nose of a twin-engined plane, such as the Japanese did with the Model 97 anti-tank rifle. This never really got a chance to show its paces because the Americans were sensible enough to cover their landing beaches with a pretty foolproof AA barrage and low-flying bombers trying to line themselves up on moving tanks were easy meat. They scored a few successes against small shipping, but even a small ship can shrug off a 20mm attack unless it hits a vital part first time. The Russians tried to overcome the failings of their twin-37mm outfit on the IL-2, which, it may be remembered, threw the plane about a bit when it fired and was positively dangerous when one gun misfired. The alternative was to fit four 23mm cannon, on the principle that the recoil force would be more evenly spread and the failure of one gun would be only half as bad as the failure of one of the 37s. The theory was good but the installation was again too heavy and this time the cannon were not really up to the job. Perhaps they might have been if the IL-2 could have delivered the shots into the roof in the same way as the Stuka, but not being a dive-bomber it couldn't. So the 23mm guns continued in their original role of AA artillery, as they still do.

Another unprofitable line of development was the one towards the bigger gun. When the 2-pounders and 37s of 1940 showed themselves in their true light, their owners demanded a bigger and more effective gun, firing a heavier shell to a longer range. They got it, and straightaway called for the next size up; and when they got that, it was time to call for the next, and so on and so on. The same process was repeated in every army with entirely predictable results. For the British it was the 32-pounder. This came about when the 17-pounder met the Royal Tigers and failed against their frontal armour. More than a little disturbed, the infantry sent up the cry for a bigger and better gun, adding a few remarks about the effectiveness of the German 88. The British answer was obvious and correct. The standard AA gun was put on to a field mounting, and this was the 3·7in. The result was a gun which would knock out any armoured vehicle ever built but was so heavy, so large and so difficult to move that the infantry recoiled from the Frankenstein they had created and only two prototypes were ever made.

It was much the same story in the other armies. The Germans produced the largest anti-tank guns of all with their PAK 44 models. These were produced in response to a specification laid down in 1944 demanding the near-incredible armour penetration of 200mm (7·8in) at 1,000m at an angle of 30°. As usual the two models were from Messrs Krupp and Rheinmetall, the Krupp version being once again on a cruciform platform like an AA gun, with a steeply sloping shield to shelter the crew. It used an electric firing mechanism which for that day was an advanced idea for anti-tank artillery. It also weighed 10 tons, which limited its value to a great extent. The shell weighed 62·4lb and left the muzzle at just over 3,000ft per second and would defeat 8in of armour at 1,000m at the stipulated 30° – hardly surprising considering its size. The Rheinmetall gun was similar in size and weight but had a few refinements such as a better balance when on its platform and a lower silhouette in action. Another good feature apparently was a bearing system between gun and platform that made it lighter and easier to traverse, but it took longer to get the gun into action than the Krupp. The German Ordnance Directorate had not given its decision on which gun it would adopt when the war ended, but one gets the impression, when reading the reports of the Allied investigators, that they at least favoured the Krupp.

The US Army got as far as a 105mm and probably a 120mm. There is at least one 105mm gun remaining so one can be sure of that, but the 120mm is more shadowy. The story goes that two were built in late 1944 and one was shipped to France for field evaluation. It was not a success and never returned. The second one was discovered a few years ago and is now languishing in the back of an arsenal somewhere but where, nobody seems to be certain. Even if the story is entirely apocryphal, it demonstrates the trend and the repulsion of the user when faced with the logical progression of his demands.

The unusual, if not the downright crackpot, appeared in the early days of the anti-tank missile age. This era stretched throughout the 1950s, with the level of wild optimism running fairly evenly all the way. It is perhaps worth noting that the first French missiles began to be generally available to the buying public in the late 1950s and from then on the rush of inventions took a more sober line as actual experience was gained with proper hardware. But with no real experience behind them, some designers were carried away by strange ideas. In 1952 the US Army Chief of Ordnance put a good deal of money into a device called Cannonball, also known as the D-40, with the intention of getting about twenty-five missiles and some associated ground equipment with which to evaluate the project.

He was backing a long-odds outsider because the D-40 had the strangest background of any anti-tank missile, for it had started life in the Navy as a submarine-launched, anti-ship weapon system. One would expect something out of the ordinary from such a beginning, and one would have been quite right. D-40 was a true ball, about 24in diameter. There were two varieties, a 300lb test model controlled by radio and a 150lb tactical version controlled by wire. The whole idea is best summed up in the words of an official document of 1955.

The D-40 is a subsonic, short range guided rocket utilizing manually operated radio or wire command guidance along a line-of-sight course. The missile may be either ground or ship launched and is propelled to the target by a solid fuel rocket exhausting through a radial jet. The missile is spherical to eliminate aerodynamic effects from the control system. Stabilization in roll, pitch and yaw, is effected by properly placed jets exhausting tangentially in response to signals from three reference gyros operating in conjunction with relays and solenoids. Guidance is achieved by applying correcting signals to shift the contact locations on the gyros, thereby changing the average orientation of the main jet and the flight of the missile.

Which puts it all into one neat package.

To expand a little on the rather bald official description, I should mention that there was one main propulsive jet and three pairs of stabilising jets. In flight the ball did not roll and it remained in the air by virtue of the fact that the main jet pointed downwards at an angle of 45° so that half of the jet's thrust supported the weight and half pushed it along. The stabilising jets maintained the delicate balancing act. It flew at 280mph to a range of 3,000yd over land, but only 1,000yd over water, taking, it

L   177

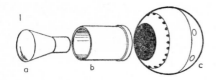

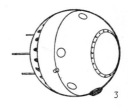

1 Exploded view of Cannonball, showing:
   a The warhead
   b The guidance pack
   c Main body and rocket motors.
2 An idealised view of Cannonball engaging a tank.
3 Cannonball complete. The three protruding probes are fuze-sensors.

should be noted, a rather leisurely 18·5 seconds to do the land journey and considerably less for the over-water flight. Guidance was by means of a joystick in the operator's hand and he sighted the target through a powerful optical system. The real merit of Cannonball lay in its warhead which was either a 50lb shaped charge or a 65lb squash head. Either was more than enough to destroy any tank that it hit. The warhead and the guidance electronics were carried in a cylinder running right through the middle of the ball, rather like the core of an apple, with an impact fuze set in the outer shell. The rocket motors were carried in the outer part of the apple, surrounding the core, and the jets were in a circle round the equator. The launch platform was a simple two-armed bracket which held the ball horizontally until it shot itself off. The Navy was concerned to have some sort of auto-loader for underwater firings.

At least fifty of these unusual missiles were fired between 1953 and 1956, all in conditions of great secrecy. They did what was expected of them and the whole programme looked most promising, but costs had risen three or four times above the original estimate, and the Army was having doubts about handling the beast in the field, so it was reluctantly dropped.

Dart was another US missile of the early 1950s, though this one was quite conventional and so similar in size and performance to the SS-11 that, when that missile came first by a year or two, Dart was abandoned. Another US idea which looked more promising was Arbalist. Arbalist was a product of the Douglas Aircraft Co, as it then still was. It was meant to overcome the main drawback of all the bazooka-type rocket-launchers, namely the low muzzle-velocity which forced the firer to aim off when his target was moving, and at all times to know the range to his target quite accurately. Douglas proposed a hyper-velocity rocket with a solid warhead using a tungsten-carbide core for the actual penetrator. There were to be no fins, simply an empty length of tube at the rear. Altogether thirty test rounds were fired. The concept was proved to be perfectly feasible provided that certain difficulties could be overcome. The penetration was excellent for a muzzle-velocity of 5,000+ft per second and the time of flight to 400yd was next to nothing, meaning that moving targets could just about be treated as if they were stationary, but the tremendous speed magnified every tiny inaccuracy as the rocket left the tube – with alarming results. Hardly any flew straight and some flew very crookedly indeed so that they all but went out of the range area altogether. The second trouble was the noise. Douglas proposed that the launcher tube should be shoulder controlled with a light tripod to steady it. The noise and blast of the rocket firing was so awesome that no human could have survived within several feet of it and it was this which killed Arbalist stone dead. A pity, it showed promise.

In Britain there appeared in the late 1950s one of the more curious proposals to ever get the blessing of the War Office. This was known by the enigmatic code name of Orange William. It was the age of coloured projects, nearly all of them destined to be victims of financial embarrassment. Blue Streak, it may be recalled, was to be a nuclear missile, and Blue Water the tactical one. Orange William was not quite an infantry weapon; it was more suited to an armoured force. In essence it was a missile with two controllers. The arrangements for it were these: the missile, which was large and conventional in appearance, with cruciform wings, was launched from a vehicle placed 2,000yd or more behind the front-line. In another vehicle very close to the front were the controllers, one watching backwards, the other forwards where he could see the target. When the forward controller wanted to fire, he called up the launch vehicle and they shot off a missile. By a complicated programme in the missile, it flew itself over the top of the controller's vehicle – an operation which demanded pin-point map reading by both vehicles – and, as it approached the area, the backwards-looking controller picked it up in his sight and guided it by radio on to a course which would start it towards the target. As the missile passed overhead, he handed over control to the forwards-looking man who then had to wait for it to appear in his field of view. When it did (if it did), he tracked it by infra-red and directed it to the target – assuming of course that the target was still there. If it was not, presumably the unfortunate controller either looked for something else, and looked pretty quickly, or just let a large and expensive missile charge off into the distance. The whole idea was hopelessly complicated and relied to an unacceptable extent upon precise teamwork from two vehicle crews separated by a mile of countryside and communicating by radio alone. Fortunately for the National Debt Orange William was squashed before any metal was cut.

10

THE FUTURE

A tank is easy prey for artillery of all calibres.

Ludendorff, 1918

Foretelling the future seems to be only profitable for gypsies and astrologers. Military writers who try their hands at it usually end up with red faces a year or two later. But one cannot leave the subject of anti-tank warfare without a timid look through the curtains of the future to see where the present trends may lead us. The way we will start is to consider the opponent, the tank, for the shape and performance of the future tank will have as much to do with future anti-tank weapons as will anything else. The first thing that strikes the eye about tanks is that they change very little with each successive year; improvements are gradual and logical, barring the few aberrations that will always crop up in any family. There has been no radical change of propulsion or shape, or offensive weaponry for several decades. A 1939 tank looks much like a 1970s tank, and uses almost the same principles in its components.

The reasons for this are not hard to find: for one thing, a tank is so expensive that it will be expected to remain in service for fifteen or more years, so, although the greatest possible advances must be made in each successive version, these advances must never go beyond what is known to be achievable and sensible. In other words, designers improve on a good design, but are cautious about too many new ideas and the result is that there is probably more conservatism in tank design than in any other branch of military equipment. One has only to look at the Soviet T-34 family to see this graphically displayed; and the British Chieftain derivation is another good example. For this reason one can say with a certain amount of confidence that for the next twenty years at least, tanks are not going to look much different from today's models. They will get faster, perhaps much faster, but here again there are distinct limits to the speed at which a vehicle weighing several tons can be driven across country and still stay in one piece, or still have a crew who can think straight. One has only to ride a motor-cycle across country to appreciate the battering the machine takes, and equally so the battering the rider would take if he were to be strapped down in a steel box instead of standing on the footrests. Armour will improve; it will have to if tanks are to survive at all, but here again it seems as if the limits are not far away and designers will have to try other avenues if more than marginal advances are going to be made. One possible idea is to reduce the size of tanks, which together with higher speeds would make them harder to detect and harder to hit. This has merit, but a small tank cannot carry a big gun and tanks are going to carry guns for several years yet. So this does not look too profitable. Armour can be made from exotic metals, titanium is one, and these are better and more efficient than steel, but they are enormously expensive to produce and difficult to weld and machine, and a modern tank needs many tons of armour.

All told therefore, it seems that, for the next generation, tanks are going to be much the same as they are today, faster perhaps, possibly smaller, but exhibiting all the characteristics of the ones in service now and carrying the same sort of armament. The only startling change may be in their ability to operate at night using electronic equipment of the kind that exists already today. However, what is available to a tank is available to the anti-tank also. The battle then becomes very much a test of who can keep awake the longest, since nightfall no longer means sleep or rest.

If the future seems more or less fixed for the tank, for a few years anyway, it is rather less so in the anti-tank field. At least as much effort is being put into improving anti-tank weapons as is ever being put into improving tanks, and because the boundaries are less easily defined in anti-tank design, the possibilities of change are far wider. But certain cautious predictions can probably be made. It is quite obvious that this is the age of the missile. Although guns still exist in large numbers, and will continue to exist, the real tank-killer is the guided missile, fired by a crew of one or two men from behind cover or from the back of a jeep, and travelling upwards of a mile before smashing the tank with an explosive warhead of such force as to put it completely out of action and turn it into a pile of scrap metal. It is a danger which the tank must now overcome, and simply thickening the armour is no longer the answer, however successful it may have been in the past. Missiles already carry enough power to defeat any armour that can be carried by a tank of reasonable weight. Any attempt to produce a thick enough plate to keep out the warhead would result in an immensely heavy vehicle which could neither manoeuvre nor cross bridges. So it seems that for the moment at least, the anti-armour school is in the lead and it is a feature of this missile superiority that many of them are carried and operated by dismounted infantry from positions on the ground. Whereas the 1945 answer to the tank was either another tank or an equally big self-propelled, anti-tank gun, the 1970s answer seems to be a solitary infantryman singlehandedly directing a lethal mass of explosive on to a selected tank with an almost certain chance of hitting it first shot.

However, before throwing the tank on to the scrap heap entirely, and throwing the anti-tank gun after it, there are a few considerations which somewhat diminish the dazzling promise of the missile. The first is cost. The missile protagonists point out that even the most expensive anti-tank missile costs only a fraction of the tank that it knocks out and this is perfectly true. Modern missiles when in mass production can be bought for $4,000–8,000 each (£2,000–3,000), which is cheap enough beside a tank costing over fifty times as much. But, as always, it is not as easy as that, and the argument only holds good if one had to buy only one missile for every tank that had to be knocked out. Unfortunately, life is never simple and soldiers have to be trained and then, having been trained, kept proficient in their acquired skills. Although there are wonderful electronic simulators which can do much for the trainee and the trained man, there is no substitute for the actual thing. Sooner or later the man has to go and fire a live missile, or maybe two; and he must continue to fire one or two every twelve months or so that he is employed as a missile operator.

Then there is the fact that he will not be an operator for all his military life. Sooner or later he will go back to civilian life, or be promoted, or simply ask for another job, and a man will have to be trained to replace him. In any case, a prudent army will already have another trained operator ready to step into his shoes should he fall sick or become a battle casualty at a crucial moment. So, rather than one missile to one tank, it begins to look as though it might be several missiles to one tank, or even many missiles and several years of peacetime readiness could make alarming inroads into the defence budget of a small country. It is not as if missiles look as if they are going to get cheaper. Electronics of the level of complexity as missiles rarely drop in price – for a parallel example, one might consider military radios which have increased in cost four or five times in the last fifteen years. There is more to it than just missiles also. The guidance equipment of some of the semi-automatic missiles is unbelievably expensive. A launcher and guidance equipment for present-day infantry anti-armour can easily cost as much as the tank it fires at, and this without adding in any missiles!

It can be seen that even the richest armies are going to use their missiles with some care and we are not yet in the age when the battlefield is going to be dotted with infantrymen licking their lips and waiting for tanks to rumble into their sights. The precious missiles will be spread comparatively thinly and moved quickly to the area of the biggest tank threat. The fastest and most efficient way of doing this is by air. Already the US Army's TOW can be mounted on a helicopter and fired while the machine is flying quite fast. This was clearly demonstrated during the closing battles of the Vietnam War when two elderly Bell UH helicopters were fitted with special missile-launchers and produced havoc among the advancing North Vietnamese tanks and armoured vehicles. There were of course tremendous advantages in favour of these helicopters – the NVA did not have any early-warning radars nor any effective AA fire, and one or two small AA missiles would have made a sharp difference to the situation – but it was the principle which was proved. An infantry anti-tank missile was carried and fired from helicopters, and this meant that it could be taken from one end of the battlefield to the other at helicopter flying speeds. This is likely to be the way that many missiles will move in the future. Not that all of them will. There will always be the place for a proportion on the ground in the forward positions.

Despite the great lethality of the missile the gun is unlikely to go out of fashion for a long time yet. It may lack the same ability to knock out tanks – and there are some who will dispute that – but tanks are not going to be the only vehicles on future battlefields. There is going to be an increasing number of armoured personnel carriers, light reconnaissance vehicles, armoured supply vehicles, command vehicles and any quantity of similar targets moving at the same time. Few of these will justify firing a valuable missile and then the gun will have to be used. A shell is a reasonably cheap munition; it can be produced in large numbers and stored for long periods without much deterioration. It can come in a variety of types, each capable of performing a different task. Anti-tank guns can, and do, not only shoot armour-piercing shot, but they can also fire HE shells which can be used against infantry, or to knock down walls, or to destroy trucks and jeeps. One would hesitate before using a missile for such targets, nor would one normally fire a missile at a suspected sniper position, but a single HE round from an anti-tank gun will do the job every time. So, while the missile takes on the serious work of engaging tanks, the gun can act in a supporting role stopping the lighter vehicles and providing some direct fire support for mundane infantry tasks. It seems a sensible division of labour.

The 1973 Arab-Israeli War has shown the appalling destruction that the missile can wreak on an opposing tank force, but it has also shown how effective is the gun once the range closes and the hard slogging match has started. The war has also shown something else – that the small one-man anti-armour weapon is still every bit as effective as were the first Panzerfausts in World War II. The Israelis have admitted that many of their tank casualties were caused by single Arab soldiers lying behind cover and waiting until a tank came sufficiently close for a certain hit with their Russian-made RPG-7 rockets. So, in addition to missiles and guns, a well-balanced anti-tank defence of the future will have to include a one-man weapon of some sort and the only worthwhile type appears to be the throw-away launcher like the M-72. These little launchers and their projectiles stretch technology to the limits in order to keep the weight to within an acceptable level, fire the projectile fast enough for accurate shooting, yet carry sufficient explosive power to damage the tank. They represent a challenge that several designers are investigating in a variety of fascinating ways. For instance, a West German arms firm recently showed an anti-tank launcher of the throw-away type that was recoilless, flashless, smokeless, and almost silent, yet fired to 300m. So far, it is still very much an experimental item, but it indicates the lengths to which inventors can go and it would be unwise to ignore it, although the idea of silent, flashless, smokeless launchers shooting to almost a quarter of a mile may seem far-fetched at the moment, stranger things have happened in space in the last decade.

BIBLIOGRAPHY

(In alphabetical order of titles)

Armoured Onslaught. Douglas Orgill. London: Ballantine Books, 1971

The Battle for Moscow 1941–42. Albert Seaton. London: Hart-Davis, 1971

The Fighting Tanks since 1916. Jones, Rarey and Icks. Washington DC: National Services Publishing, 1933

German Aircraft Guns and Cannons of World War II. Edward Hoffschmidt. New York: WE, 1969

German Defense Tactics against Russian Breakthroughs. Washington DC: US Department of the Army Historical Division, 1951

German Infantry Weapons. US Department of the Army, 1943; repr Normount Armament Co, 1966

German Tank and Anti-Tank of World War II. Edward Hoffschmidt. New York: WE, 1969

The Guns 1914–18. Ian V. Hogg. London: Ballantine Books, 1972

The Guns 1939–45. Ian V. Hogg. London: Ballantine Books, 1971

Hard Pounding. Lt-Colonel G. D. W. Court, MC. Fort Sill, Okla: US Field Artillery Association, 1945

The High Speed Internal Combustion Engine. Sir Harry Ricardo and J. Glyde. London: Blackie, 1922

Jackets of Green. Arthur Bryant. London: Collins, 1972

Jane's Weapon Systems. R. Pretty and D. Archer. London: British Publishing Corporation, 1972

Japanese Combat Weapons. E. Hoffschmidt and A. Tatum. New York: WE, 1969

Japanese Infantry Weapons. US Department of the Army, 1943; repr Normount Armament Co, 1966

Military Improvisation during the Russian Campaign. Washington DC: US Department of the Army Historical Division, 1952

No Parachute. Arthur Gould-Lee. New York: Harper & Row, 1972

Operations of Encircled Forces. Washington DC: US Department of the Army Historical Division, 1952

The Other Side of the Hill. B. L. Liddell-Hart. London: Cassells, 1951

The Other War. Donovan Ward. Birmingham: BSA Ltd, 1946

Russian Combat Methods in World War II. Washington DC: US Department of the Army Historical Division, 1956

Small Unit Actions in the Russian Campaign. Washington DC: US Department of the Army Historical Division, 1953

The Spanish Civil War. Hugh Thomas. London: Eyre & Spottiswoode, 1961

Stuka Pilot. Hans Rudel. New York: Ballantine Books, 1964

The Tank Destroyer History. Washington DC: US Army Historical Section, Army Ground Forces, 1946

The Tanks, Vols 1–2. B. L. Liddell-Hart. London: Cassells, 1959

Truppendienst Taschenbuche, 1–3. Vienna: Verlag Carl Uberreuter, 1969

US Military Vehicles in World War II. E. Hoffschmidt and A. Tatum. New York: WE, 1970

ACKNOWLEDGEMENTS

One cannot write a book of this kind without help. I have needed more than most, but in calling for it I have been unusually fortunate, for I have never been refused, never been turned away with a surly answer, never given second-best information, and never asked for any payment. It has all been a most heartening experience which has put me in touch with a circle of friends stretching half-way across the world, friends who were never too busy to answer my letters, take my telephone calls, search their files and attics, phone up other friends, give me a bed for the night when I was stranded, or, as occasionally happened, lend me their car. One day I may be able to repay them, but it seems unlikely. The following list is inevitably incomplete and to those who do not appear in it, I can only offer my sincere apologies.

My gratitude goes out to the following:

To Edward Hoffschmidt of Stamford, Connecticut, who once entertained me for a whole evening in his house and has many times since brightened a weary day with his pungent and amusing letters. I turned to him for many of the illustrations for this book, and he has also made some of the drawings.

To Hal Johnston of Fairfax, Virginia, whose encouragement and support has been continuous. His extensive library was always at my disposal and his recollections of a life spent among weapons has been a constant source of delight and education for me.

To Mr Steve Costner of the United States Marine Corps Museum in Quantico, who on more than one occasion patiently helped me ruin the order and cleanliness of his warehouse so that I could take photographs of his rarer pieces.

To Colonel Mitchell Sharpe of Redstone Arsenal, who unfailingly turned up the reference to everything I asked for and even persuaded the United States Navy to declassify some documents for me to use in this book.

To the late Colonel Burling Jarrett of Aberdeen, Maryland, who knew more about this subject than I shall ever learn, and who should have written this book. His memory was phenomenal, his kindness endless, and his scholarship renowned.

To Mr Hoskins of the Air Historical Branch of the Ministry of Defence for his information on the Hurricane IID.

To Mr Durant of the Smithsonian Institution in Washington for his help over early rocket experiments.

To Mrs Goddard for her permission to publish the photographs of her late husband, the noted rocket pioneer, Dr Goddard.

To Bob Fisch of the West Point Museum for his photograph.

To Major Freddie Myatt of the Weapon Museum, Warminster, Wiltshire, for permission to photograph his exhibits, use his library, and copy his stock of pamphlets.

To the library staff of the Ministry of Defence, London, for their research on my behalf, as a result of which I was able to write the majority of Chapter 3.

To the Historian and museum staff of Picatinny Arsenal, New Jersey.

To the museum staff of Aberdeen Proving Ground, Maryland, for their patience and assistance.

To the Imperial War Museum for the use of their photographs.

To the ladies of the Pentagon Audio-Visual Library for their cheerfulness and help with my curious questions.

To Dave Harris of Redstone Arsenal for permission to draw on his article about the early history of the Bazooka.

To Shirley Thomas, who typed, retyped, and typed yet again the script, interpreting my extraordinary mangled drafts, correcting my spelling, punctuating and querying the obscure passages. She has done more than anyone to get this book to the presses.

And finally, to my wife, who on being told that I was about to write this book, exclaimed, 'Good God, that means another six months when we can't use the family room', but who unflaggingly supported me and brought the whisky when the evenings began to drag.

INDEX